THE PASSION TRANSLATION

2020 edition

letters from heaven

INCLUDES THE BOOKS OF

GALATIANS,
EPHESIANS,
PHILIPPIANS,
COLOSSIANS,
1 & 2 THESSALONIANS,
1 & 2 TIMOTHY,
TITUS,
PHILEMON

BroadStreet
P U B L I S H I N G

The Passion Translation®
Galatians, Ephesians, Philippians, Colossians, 1 & 2 Thessalonians, 1 & 2 Timothy, Titus, and Philemon: Letters from Heaven

Published by BroadStreet Publishing® Group, LLC
BroadStreetPublishing.com
ThePassionTranslation.com

For information about bulk sales or customized editions of The Passion Translation, please contact orders@broadstreetpublishing.com.

The publisher and TPT team have worked diligently and prayerfully to present this version of The Passion Translation Bible with excellence and accuracy. If you find a mistake in the Bible text or footnotes, please contact the publisher at tpt@broadstreetpublishing.com.

978-1-4245-6332-6 (paperback)
978-1-4245-6333-3 (e-book)

Printed in China

21 22 23 24 25 5 4 3 2 1

CONTENTS

A NOTE TO READERS

It would be impossible to calculate how many lives have been changed forever by the power of the Bible, the living Word of God! My own life was transformed because I believed the message contained in Scripture about Jesus, the Savior.

To hold the Bible dear to your heart is the sacred obsession of every true follower of Jesus. Yet to go even further and truly understand the Bible is how we gain light and truth to live by. Did you catch the word *understand*? People everywhere say the same thing: "I want to understand God's Word, not just read it."

Thankfully, as English speakers, we have a plethora of Bible translations, commentaries, study guides, devotionals, churches, and Bible teachers to assist us. Our hearts crave to know God—to not just know about him, but to know him as intimately as we possibly can in this life. This is what makes Bible translations so valuable, because each one will hopefully lead us into new discoveries of God's character. I believe God is committed to giving us truth in a package we can understand and apply, so I thank God for every translation of God's Word that we have.

God's Word does not change, but over time languages definitely do, thus the need for updated and revised translations of the Bible. Translations give us the words God spoke through his servants, but words can be poor containers for revelation because they leak! Meaning is influenced by culture, background, and many other details. Just imagine how differently the Hebrew authors of the Old Testament saw the world three thousand years ago from the way we see it today!

Even within one language and culture, meanings of words change from one generation to the next. For example, many contemporary Bible readers would be quite surprised to find unicorns are mentioned nine times in the King James Version (KJV). Here's one instance in Isaiah 34:7: "And the unicorns shall come down with them, and the bullocks with the bulls; and their land shall be soaked with blood, and their dust made fat with fatness." This isn't a result of poor translation, but rather an example of how our culture, language, and understanding of the world has shifted over the past few centuries. So, it is important that we have a modern English text of the Bible that releases revelation and truth into our hearts. The Passion Translation (TPT) is committed to bringing forth the potency of God's Word in relevant, contemporary vocabulary that doesn't distract from its meaning or distort it in any way. So many people have told us that they are falling in love with the Bible again as they read TPT.

We often hear the statement, "I just want a word-for-word translation that doesn't mess it up or insert a bias." That's a noble desire. But a word-for-word translation would be nearly unreadable. It is simply impossible to translate one Hebrew word for one English word. Hebrew is built from triliteral consonant roots. Biblical Hebrew had no vowels or punctuation. And Koine Greek, although wonderfully articulate, cannot always be conveyed in English by a word-for-word translation. For example, a literal word-for-word translation of the Greek in Matthew 1:18 would be something like this: "Of the but Jesus Christ the birth thus was. Being betrothed the mother of him, Mary, to Joseph, before or to come together them she was found in belly having from Spirit Holy."

Even the KJV, which many believe to be a very literal translation, renders this verse: "Now the birth of Jesus Christ was on this wise: When as his mother Mary was espoused to Joseph, before they came together, she was found with child of the Holy Ghost."

This comparison makes the KJV look like a paraphrase next to a strictly literal translation! To some degree, every Bible translator is forced to move words around in a sentence to convey with meaning the thought of the verse. There is no such thing as a truly literal translation of the Bible, for there is not an equivalent language that perfectly conveys the meaning of the biblical text. Is it really possible to have a highly accurate and highly readable English Bible? We certainly hope so! It is so important that God's Word is living in our hearts, ringing in our ears, and burning in our souls. Transferring God's revelation from Hebrew and Greek into English is an art, not merely a linguistic science. Thus, we need all the accurate translations we can find. If a verse or passage in one translation seems confusing, it is good to do a side-by-side comparison with another version.

It is difficult to say which translation is the "best." "Best" is often in the eyes of the reader and is determined by how important differing factors are to different people. However, the "best" translation, in my thinking, is the one that makes the Word of God clear and accurate, no matter how many words it takes to express it.

That's the aim of The Passion Translation: to bring God's eternal truth into a highly readable heart-level expression that causes truth and love to jump out of the text and lodge inside our hearts. A desire to remain accurate to the text and a desire to communicate God's heart of passion for his people are the two driving forces behind TPT. So for those new to Bible reading, we hope TPT will excite and illuminate. For scholars and Bible students, we hope TPT will bring the joys of new discoveries from the text and prompt deeper consideration of what God has spoken to his people. We all have so much more to learn and discover about God in his holy Word!

You will notice at times we've italicized certain words or phrases. These portions are not in the original Hebrew, Greek, or Aramaic manuscripts but are implied from the context. We've made these implications explicit for the sake of narrative clarity and to better convey the meaning of God's Word. This is a common practice by mainstream translations.

We've also chosen to translate certain names in their original Hebrew or Greek forms to better convey their cultural meaning and significance. For instance, some translations of the Bible have substituted James for Jacob and Jude for Judah. Both Greek and Aramaic manuscripts leave these Hebrew names in their original forms. Therefore, this translation uses those cultural names.

The purpose of The Passion Translation is to reintroduce the passion and fire of the Bible to the English reader. It doesn't merely convey the literal meaning of words. It expresses God's passion for people and his world by translating the original, life-changing message of God's Word for modern readers.

We pray this version of God's Word will kindle in you a burning desire to know the heart of God, while impacting the church for years to come.

Please visit **ThePassionTranslation.com** for more information.

Brian Simmons and the translation team

GALATIANS

Introduction

AT A GLANCE

Author: The apostle Paul
Audience: The church of Galatia
Date: AD 47–48, or early 50s
Type of Literature: A letter
Major Themes: Grace gospel, justification, the law, legalism, freedom and behavior, and Jesus Christ
Outline:
  Letter Opening — 1:1–10
  Paul Defends His Ministry and Message — 1:11–2:21
  Paul Defends His Theology and Gospel — 3:1–4:31
  Paul Applies His Message Practically — 5:1–6:10
  Letter Closing — 6:11–18

ABOUT GALATIANS

Heaven's freedom! This "grace gospel" brings heaven's freedom into our lives—freedom to live for God and serve one another, as well as freedom from religious bondage. We can thank God today that Paul's gospel is still being preached and heaven's freedom is available to every believer. We are free to soar even higher than keeping religious laws; we have a grace-righteousness that places us at the right hand of the throne of God, not as servants, but as sons and daughters of the Most High!

When Paul wrote his letter, the grace gospel was under attack. So too was his apostolic ministry—it was also debunked by those who wanted to mix grace with the keeping of Jewish law. Paul begins his letter to the Galatians by making it clear that it was not a group of men who commissioned him; instead, he was a "sent one" by the direct commissioning of our Lord Jesus Christ. And the message of grace that he preached was not a secondhand truth that he got from someone else, for he received it through a direct encounter with Jesus. Paul's ministry can be trusted and his gospel can be believed.

Who was this man, Paul? He was born with the name Saul in the city of Tarsus, the once prosperous capital of Cilicia in southern Turkey. Apparently there was a large Jewish colony in that region. Yet Saul was raised in Jerusalem and tutored by the venerated Jewish rabbi Gamaliel.

Before Saul was converted through a divine encounter, he was considered one of the most brilliant Jewish Pharisees of his day. After his conversion to Christ, however, his name became Paul and his ministry began. Reaching the non-Jewish nations with the glorious gospel of Christ was Paul's passion and pursuit. We can thank God that this brilliant man has left us his inspired letters to the churches.

PURPOSE

What a wonderful purpose is found in this letter from heaven! Shortly after the Holy Spirit was poured out upon Jewish believers in Yeshua (Jesus), the gospel spread to other ethnicities as well. By the apostolic mandate given to Jesus' disciples, they were sent into every nation. The first converts among the non-Jewish people needed clarity as to the "Jewishness" of the gospel. Was the gospel revelation to be based upon grace or upon keeping the law of Moses? Galatians was written by the apostle Paul to put those questions to rest.

AUTHOR AND AUDIENCE

The chronological order of the books of the New Testament is somewhat certain. However, the first book Paul wrote is often debated; some say it was 1 Thessalonians and others claim it was Galatians. It is my conclusion that Galatians was the first book he penned, possibly around AD 47–48, in order to passionately defend the gospel of grace from those who would confuse and twist the truth. The apostolic burden is always for purity, both in doctrine and in practice, which is why he confronted those who were distorting the gospel of Christ and reminded the Galatian church of the true message of grace.

MAJOR THEMES

Grace Gospel. When Paul wrote his letter proclaiming heaven's freedom, there were people perverting his original message of rescue from sin and death by grace through faith in Christ alone. These Judaizers, as they were called, added religious works to Paul's gospel, which placed non-Jewish believers under the thumb of religious bondage to Jewish laws. Thanks to Paul, we are reminded that a Christ-plus-something-gospel is no gospel at all; it is Christ-plus-nothing all the way!

Justification. One of the central issues for Paul in Galatians—and throughout his "Letters from Heaven"—is the issue of how people become right with God and find a "not guilty" verdict for their rebellion against him. The Reformation leader Martin Luther said that justification by grace through faith was the belief by which the church stands or falls. He's right! And Paul explains how it's possible a person can stand before a holy God without being condemned.

The Law and Legalism. The message of Galatians is clear: Christ's redemptive work on the cross prevents Jews and non-Jews alike from trying to become right with God through religious works; rescue and re-creation come on the basis of faith in Jesus alone. Through his grace, we are freed from the religious bondage that comes from laws and rituals.

Freedom and Behavior. The grace gospel brings heaven's freedom from religious bondage. Yet while Christians are free from the law, we are not free to live as we please. Instead, we are called to use that freedom to produce fruit, the "fruit of the Spirit," as Paul says. And it is through the Spirit of God that we not only find freedom but are also empowered to please God with our behavior.

Jesus Christ. As you might expect in a letter about salvation, Jesus Christ stands at the center of this letter. We see that Jesus is fully divine and should alone be worshiped. His cross also plays a pivotal role in Paul's grace-letter, for it is through his sacrifice alone that believers are made right with God.

GALATIANS

Heaven's Freedom

Introduction

1 From Paul,[a] an apostle[b] of Jesus Christ. My apostleship was not granted to me by men, for I was appointed by Jesus Christ, and God the Father, who raised him from the dead. [2]All the brothers and sisters[c] join with me as I

---

a 1:1 The name Paul means "little." His name before his conversion was Saul, which means "significant one" or "sought after." What great transformation takes place when we experience a profound change as Saul did! God transforms us from being "important" to being "small" in our own eyes. This is what qualifies God's apostolic servants.

b 1:1 The word *apostle* means "one who is sent on a mission" or "an ambassador." By implication, an apostle carries the delegated authority of the one who sends him. Jesus Christ chose Paul to be an apostle to plant churches and impart the revelation of Christ and his true gospel. The New Testament refers more often to the gift of apostle than all the other ascension gifts (prophet, evangelist, pastor, and teacher) combined. See Eph. 4:11.

c 1:2 The Greek word *adelphos* is used throughout the New Testament for brothers (and sisters). It is used in classical Greek by physicians to describe "those who came from the same womb." Every believer is born from the same "womb" of the Father's heart and the wounded side of Jesus Christ. In the time of Alexander the Great, the word *adelphos* was used not only for brothers (and sisters), but for "faithful soldiers." How wonderful it is in our journey to know that we have partners in battle fighting for the faith alongside of us.

write this letter to the churches throughout the region of central Turkey.[a]

[3]May God's undeserved kindness and total well-being[b] that flow from our Father God and from the Lord Jesus be yours.[c] [4]He's the Anointed One who offered himself *as the sacrifice* for our sins! He has rescued us from this evil world system[d] and set us free, just as our Father God desired. [5]May all the glory be to God alone, throughout time and eternity. Amen!

One Gospel

[6]I am shocked over how quickly you have strayed away from the One who called you in the grace of Christ. I'm astounded that you now embrace a distorted[e] gospel! [7]That is a fake "gospel" that is simply not true. There is only one gospel—the good news of Christ! Yet you have allowed those who mingle law with grace to confuse you.

[8]But even if we or an angel from heaven should preach a gospel different than the one we preached to you, let them be under God's curse!

---

a 1:2 Or "Galatia." This was the region in Asia Minor (modern-day Turkey) that Paul visited during his first and second missionary journeys. See Acts 16:1–5.

b 1:3 This is the word *peace*, which in the Hebraic mindset means "health, prosperity, peace, and total well-being." The phrase *grace and peace* appears as a greeting in Rom. 1:7, 1 Cor. 1:3, 2 Cor. 1:2, Gal. 1:3, Eph. 1:2, Phil. 1:2, Col. 1:2, 1 Thess. 1:1, 2 Thess. 1:2, Titus 1:4, 1 Peter 1:2, 2 Peter 1:2, and Rev. 1:4.

c 1:3 Grace was not just a "message" that Paul taught; it was the way he dealt with deceived people. Even over the confused churches that were mixing works and grace, Paul spoke words of blessing and peace. When we learn to bless and release "undeserved kindness" and "well-being" over those who oppose us, perhaps then they will listen to us.

d 1:4 This "evil world system" would include the religious system that is based on duty and performance instead of love and grace.

e 1:6 Or "another gospel."

⁹Let me make it clear: Anyone, no matter who they are, that brings you a different gospel than the gospel that you have received, let them be condemned and cursed!

¹⁰I'm obviously not trying to flatter you or water down my message to be popular with men, but my supreme passion is to please God. For if all I attempt to do is please people, I would fail to be a true servant of Christ.

How Paul Became an Apostle

¹¹Beloved ones, let me repeat emphatically that the gospel entrusted to me was not given to me by any man. ¹²No one taught me this revelation, for it was given to me directly by the unveiling of Jesus Christ.

¹³By now you have heard stories of how severely[a] I harassed and persecuted Christians and how systematically I endeavored to destroy God's church, all because of my radical devotion to the Jewish religion.[b] ¹⁴My zeal and passion for the doctrines of Judaism distinguished me among my people, for I was far more advanced in my religious instruction than others my age.

¹⁵But then God called me by his grace, and chose me from my birth to be his. ¹⁶He was pleased to unveil his Son in me so that I would proclaim him to the peoples of the world. After I had this encounter, I kept it a secret for some time, sharing it with no one. ¹⁷And I had no desire to run to Jerusalem and try to impress those who had become apostles before me. Instead, I withdrew into the Arabian Desert. Then I returned to Damascus, *where I had first encountered Jesus.* ¹⁸I remained there for three years until I eventually went up to Jerusalem, met the apostle

---

a 1:13 The Aramaic can be translated "beyond measure."

b 1:13 The Jewish way of life includes not only religion but also culture. Paul is using the word *religion* broadly, not only to include the rich culture of Judaism, but also to include the various religious traditions not found in the Torah.

Peter,[a] and stayed with him for a couple of weeks. [19]The only other apostle I met during that time was Jacob,[b] the Lord's brother.

[20]Everything I'm describing to you I confess before God to be the absolute truth. [21]After my stay in Jerusalem, I went to Syria and southeast Turkey,[c] [22]but I remained unknown to the churches[d] in Judea. [23]The only thing they heard about me was this: "Our former enemy, who once brutally persecuted us, is now preaching the good news of the faith that he tried to destroy!" [24]*Because of the transformation that took place in my life*, they praised God even more!

Church Leaders Accept Paul as an Apostle

2 Fourteen years later, I returned to Jerusalem, this time with Barnabas[e] and Titus,[f] *my coworkers*. [2]*God gave me a clear revelation[g] to go and confer with the other apostles concerning the message of grace I was preaching to the gentiles. I spoke privately with those who were viewed as senior leaders of the church, wanting to make certain that my labor and ministry for the Messiah had not been based on a false understanding of the gospel.[h]

---

a 1:18 The Aramaic name of Peter is *kefa*, which means "rock."

b 1:19 Or "James." However, his true name was not James, but Jacob. See the introduction to the book of James (Jacob).

c 1:21 Or "Cilicia," which was the southeastern province of Asia Minor, directly adjoining Syria.

d 1:22 Today we would call these Jewish believers in Messiah "Messianic Jews"—not only Jewish (by birth) but also Christian (by faith).

e 2:1 Barnabas is an Aramaic name that means "son of encouragement."

f 2:1 Titus was a gentile convert to Christ and was a frequent companion of Paul's. Later Paul wrote a beautiful letter to Titus. Titus' name means "nurse."

g 2:2 Although we don't know exactly what the "clear revelation" might have been, it is possible it came in the form of a dream, a vision, a prophecy, or an angel that appeared to Paul.

h 2:2 Or "to make sure I was not running the race for nothing."

³Even though Titus*ª* was a Syrian,*ᵇ* *they accepted him as a brother* without demanding that he first be circumcised. *⁴I met with them privately* because false "brothers" had been secretly smuggled into church meetings. They were sent to spy on the *wonderful* freedom that we have in Jesus Christ. Their agenda was to bring us back into the bondage *of religion.* ⁵But you must know that we did not submit to their religious shackles,*ᶜ* not even for a moment, so that we might keep the truth of the gospel *of grace* unadulterated for you.

⁶Even those most influential among the brothers were not able to add anything to my message. Who they are before men makes no difference to me, for God is not impressed by their reputations.*ᵈ* ⁷So they recognized that I was entrusted with taking the gospel to the gentiles*ᵉ* just as Peter was entrusted with taking it to the Jews.*ᶠ* ⁸For the same God who empowered Peter's apostolic ministry to the Jews also flowed through me as an apostle to those who are gentiles.

⁹When they all recognized this grace operating in my ministry, those who were recognized as influential pillars*ᵍ* in the church—Jacob, Peter, and John—extended to

---

a 2:3 Titus was converted through Paul's ministry and was later sent out by Paul as an apostolic church planter. The book of Titus was written by Paul to his spiritual son to give him encouragement and revelation for his ministry.

b 2:3 Or "Aramean," which is an Aramaic-speaking gentile. Syrians are Arameans, but Greeks are not. Most Greek manuscripts identify Titus as a Greek when, in fact, he was Syrian. It is believed that the Greek scribes changed Titus' ethnicity to Greek, but the Aramaic text correctly identifies him as a Syrian.

c 2:5 Or in Aramaic "their efforts to enslave us" or "their oppression."

d 2:6 Or "God does not accept the face (mask) of a man."

e 2:7 Or "the uncircumcised."

f 2:7 Or "the circumcised."

g 2:9 See Rev. 3:12.

Barnabas and me the warmth of Christian fellowship[a] and honored my calling to *minister to* the gentiles, even as they were to go to the Jews. [10]They simply requested one thing of me: that I would remember the poor and needy, which was the burden I was already carrying in my heart.

Paul Confronts Peter

[11]When Peter visited Antioch,[b] he *caused the believers to stumble over his behavior*, so I confronted him to his face. [12]He enjoyed eating with the gentile believers who didn't keep the Jewish customs—up until the time Jacob's Jewish friends arrived from Jerusalem. When he saw them, he withdrew from his gentile friends—fearing how it would look to them[c] *if he ate with gentile believers*.

[13]And so, because of Peter's hypocrisy,[d] many other Jewish believers followed suit, refusing to eat with gentile believers. Even Barnabas was led astray by their hypocritical behavior!

[14]So when I realized they were acting inconsistently with the revelation of the gospel, I confronted Peter in front of everyone:

"You were born a Jew, but you've chosen to disregard Jewish regulations and live like a gentile.[e] Why then do you force gentiles to conform to these same rules?"

---

a 2:9 Or "gave me the right hand of fellowship."

b 2:11 Antioch was a large city in Syria with a significant Jewish population. It was in Antioch that believers were first called Christians and it was the first church to send out missionaries to the nations. See Acts 11:25–26; 13:1–3.

c 2:12 Or "fearing those of the circumcision."

d 2:13 The incident of Acts 10–11 happened before this account in Gal. 2. Peter was shown by a heavenly vision that God views gentile believers as "clean." This amplifies Peter's hypocrisy. Even Jesus' apostles had conflicts that needed to be worked out and healed.

e 2:14 Some Aramaic translators translate this word "Syrian" or "Aramean."

Jews and Gentiles Are Saved by Faith

¹⁵Although we're Jews by birth and not gentile "sinners," ¹⁶we know that no one receives God's perfect righteousness as a reward for keeping the law, but only by the faith of Jesus, the Messiah!ᵃ His faithfulness has saved us, and we have received God's perfect righteousness. Now we know that God accepts no one by the keeping of *religious* laws!ᵇ

¹⁷If we are those who desire to be righteous through our union with the Anointed One, does that mean our Messiah condones sin even though we acknowledge that we are sinners? How absurd! ¹⁸For if I start over and reconstruct the old religious system that I had torn down *with the message of grace*, I would appear to be a lawbreaker.ᶜ

¹⁹For through the law I died to the law,ᵈ so that I might live to God.ᵉ

²⁰My old identity has been co-crucified with Christ and no longer lives. And now the essence of this new life is no longer mine, for the Anointed One lives his life through me—*we live in union as one!*ᶠ My new life is empowered by the faith of the Son of God who loves me so much that he gave himself for me, *dispensing his life into mine!*

²¹So that is why I don't view God's grace as something peripheral.ᵍ For if keeping the law could release God's righteousness to us, then Christ would have died for nothing.

---

a 2:16 The Aramaic and Greek can be translated "the faith *of* Jesus, the Messiah" or "faith *in* Jesus Christ." It is not simply our faith, but his— the faithfulness of Jesus to fulfill the Father's pleasure in his life and the sacrifice for our sins in his death. Salvation is found in the "faith of Jesus."

b 2:16 Or "by the works of the law."

c 2:18 Or "I prove myself to be a sinner."

d 2:19 See Rom. 6:2; 7:4.

e 2:19 See Rom. 6:10, 11, 14; 2 Cor. 5:15.

f 2:20 We are one with him, and he lives in us. See John 14:20.

g 2:21 Or "I do not nullify the grace of God (by adding works)."

Faith Brings Freedom

3 What has happened to you foolish Galatians? Who has put you under an evil spell?[a] Did God not open your eyes to see the meaning of Jesus' crucifixion? Was he not revealed to you as the crucified one?[b]

[2]So answer me this: Did the Holy Spirit come to you as a reward for keeping *Jewish laws*? No, you received him as a gift because you believed in the Messiah. [3]Your new life began when the Holy Spirit gave you a new birth. Why then would you so foolishly turn from living in the Spirit by trying to finish by your own works?[c]

[4]Have you endured so many trials and persecutions for nothing?

[5]Let me ask you again: What does the lavish supply of the Holy Spirit in your life and the miracles of God's tremendous power have to do with you keeping religious laws? The Holy Spirit is poured out upon us through the revelation and power of faith!

[6]Abraham, *our father of faith*, believed God, and the substance of his faith released God's righteousness to him.[d] [7]So the true children of Abraham have the same faith as their father! [8]And the Scripture prophesied that on the basis of faith God would declare gentiles to be righteous. God announced the good news ahead of time to Abraham:

"Through your example of faith, all the nations will be blessed!"[e]

---

a 3:1 The Greek word used here means "to cast a spell using the evil eye." Paul uses a pun here in the Greek text. He goes on to say, "Didn't God *open* your *eyes*?"

b 3:1 The great revelation of the cross had been supernaturally given to them; but they were diluting the glorious work of the cross by adding to it the works of religion.

c 3:3 As translated from the Aramaic.

d 3:6 See Gen. 15:6.

e 3:8 See Gen. 12:3; 18:18; 22:18.

⁹And so the blessing of Abraham's faith is now our blessing too! ¹⁰But if you rely on works of keeping the law *for salvation*, you live under the law's curse. For it is clearly written:

> "Utterly cursed is everyone who fails to practice
> every detail and requirement that is written in this
> law!"ᵃ

¹¹It is obvious that no one achieves the righteousness of God by attempting to keep the law, for it is written:

> "The one who is in a right relationship with God will
> live by faith!"ᵇ

¹²But keeping the law does not require faith, *but self-effort*. For the law teaches,

> "If you practice the principles of law, you must
> follow all of them."ᶜ

¹³Yet, Christ paid the full price to set us free from the curse of the law. He absorbed the curse completely as he became a curse in our place. For it is written:

> "Everyone who is hung upon a tree is cursed."ᵈ

¹⁴Jesus Christ dissolved the curse from our lives, so that in him all the blessings of Abraham can be poured out upon gentiles. And now through faith we receive the promised Holy Spirit *who lives in us*.

---

a 3:10 See Deut. 27:26.
b 3:11 See Hab. 2:4.
c 3:12 See Lev. 18:5.
d 3:13 See Deut. 21:23.

The Law versus God's Promises

[15]Beloved friends, let me use an illustration that we can all understand. Technically, when a contract is signed, it can't be changed after it has been put into effect; it's too late to alter the agreement.[a]

[16]Remember the royal proclamation[b] God spoke over Abraham and to Abraham's child? God said that his promises were made to pass on to Abraham's "Child,"[c] not children. And who is this "Child?" It's *the Son of promise,* Christ himself!

[17-18]This means that the covenant between God and Abraham was fulfilled in Messiah and cannot be altered. Yet the written law was not even given to Moses until 430 years after God had "signed" his contract with Abraham! The law, then, doesn't supersede the promise[d] since the royal proclamation was given before the law.[e]

If that were the case, it would have nullified what God said to Abraham. We receive all the promises because of the Promised One—not because we keep the law!

[19]Why then was the law given at all? It was given alongside the promise to show people their sins. But the law was designed to last only until the coming of the "Seed," the child who was promised. When God gave the law, he gave it first to angels; they gave it to *Moses,* his mediator, who then gave it to the people. [20]Now, a mediator does

---

a 3:15 The most ancient Aramaic manuscript has a different meaning for this verse. It could also be translated, "The covenant of the Son of Man that I reference should never be denigrated or changed in any way by men."

b 3:16 As translated literally from the Greek. It can also mean "covenant."

c 3:16 Or "seed."

d 3:17–18 The concept of the "promise" is that all we need is faith to believe it. This is the revelation of grace that saves us, for the "promise" is enough.

e 3:17–18 This last sentence is the implied conclusion of Paul's logic.

not represent just one party alone, but God fulfilled it all by himself![a]

[21]Since that's true, should we consider the written law to be contrary to the promise of new life? How absurd![b] Truly, if there was a law that we could keep which would give us new life, then our salvation would have come by law-keeping. [22]But the Scriptures make it clear that the whole world is imprisoned by sin! This was so the promise would be given through faith to people who believe in Jesus Christ.

God's Sons Inherit the Promises

[23]So until the revelation of faith for salvation was released, the law was a jailer, holding us as prisoners under lock and key until the "faith," which was destined to be revealed, *would set us free.* [24]The law was our guardian until Christ came so that we would be saved by faith. [25]But now that faith has come[c] we are no longer under the guardian *of the law.*

[26]You have all become true children of God by faith in Jesus Christ! [27]Faith immersed you into Christ, and now you are covered and clothed with his life. [28]And we no longer see each other *in our former state*—Jew or non-Jew, rich or poor,[d] male or female—because we're all one through our union with Jesus Christ.

---

a 3:20 Or "but God is one."

b 3:21 The law and the promise (grace) each have a distinct function. The law brings conviction of sin, which unveils grace as the way to salvation. The law moves us, even compels us, to reach for grace. And grace will cause one to soar even higher than the demands of the law.

c 3:25 Or "But now that Faith has come," a title for the Lord Jesus (Faith).

d 3:28 Or "enslaved or free."

²⁹And if you belong to Christ, then you are now Abraham's "child" and a true heir of all his blessings because of the promise *God made to Abraham*!

From Slavery to Sonship

4 Let me illustrate: As long as an heir is a minor, he's not really much different than a servant, although he's the master over all of them. ²For until the time appointed by the father, the child is under the domestic supervision of the guardians of the estate.

³So it is with us. When we were juveniles we were enslaved under the hostile spirits of the world. ⁴But when the time of fulfillment had come, God sent his Son, born of a woman,ᵃ born under the law. ⁵Yet all of this was so that he would redeem and set free those held hostage to the law so that we would receive our freedom and a full legal adoption as his children.

⁶And so that we would know that we are his true children,ᵇ God released the Spirit of Sonship into our hearts—moving us to cry out intimately, "My Father!ᶜ My true Father!"

⁷Now we're no longer living like slaves *under the law*, but we enjoy being God's very own sons and daughters! And because we're his, *we can access everything our Father has*—for we are heirs because of what God has done!

---

a 4:4 Every child has a mother; but for Jesus to be "born of a woman" meant there was no human father, no male counterpart. Jesus' true Father is the Father of Eternity. No other child has had a virgin birth, "born of a woman," except him. All the rest of us are born from a father and a mother.

b 4:6 Or "because you are sons."

c 4:6 This is the Aramaic word *Abba* which means "my father." *Abba* was borrowed by the Greeks and is found in the Greek manuscripts as well.

⁸Before we knew God *as our Father*, we were unwitting servants to the powers that be, which are nothing compared to God. ⁹But now that we truly know him and are intimately known by him, why would we for a moment consider turning back to those weak and feeble principles of religion, as though we were still subject to them?

¹⁰Why would we want to scrupulously observe rituals like special days,ᵃ celebrations of the new moon, annual festivals, and sacred years?ᵇ ¹¹I'm so alarmed about you that I'm beginning to wonder if my labor in ministry among you was a waste of time!

Paul's Personal Appeal

¹²Beloved ones, I plead with you, brothers and sisters, become like me, for I became like you. You did me no wrong.

¹³You are well aware that the reason I stayed among you to preach the good news was because of the poor state of my health.ᶜ ¹⁴And yet you were so kind to me and did not despise me in my weakness,ᵈ even though my physical condition put you through an ordeal while I was with you.

---

a 4:10 Or "Sabbaths." There is no requirement for gentiles to become like Jews and observe Jewish ordinances in order to draw closer to God. Our approach to God is always on the basis of grace and faith in the blood of Jesus Christ, the Lord of the Sabbath.

b 4:10 These terms could also apply to following astrological signs.

c 4:13 Paul's ministry in Antioch began when he became sick and had to delay his missionary journey to other regions. He may have been afflicted with an illness, or an ophthalmic disorder that was prevalent in the region. The disorder can cause one to have a repugnant appearance. Other scholars think he was simply very ill as a result of his treatment by his enemies on his first missionary journey. Still the Galatians did not reject him; instead they welcomed him with open arms, and his gospel message with open hearts.

d 4:14 The Aramaic word can also mean "sickness."

Actually, you received me and cared for me as though I were an angel from God, as you would have cared for Jesus Christ himself! [15]Some of you were even willing, if it were possible, to pluck out your own eyes to replace mine! Where is that kindhearted and free spirit now? [16]Have I really become your enemy because I tell you the truth?

[17]Can't you see what these false teachers[a] are doing? They want to win you over so you will side with them. They want you divided from me so you will follow only them. Would you call that integrity? [18]Isn't it better to seek excellence and integrity always, and not just only when I'm with you?

[19]You are my dear children, but I agonize in spiritual "labor pains" once again, until the Anointed One will be fully formed in your hearts! [20]How I wish I could be there in person and change my tone toward you, for I am truly dumbfounded over what you are doing!

An Old Testament Allegory

[21-22]Tell me, do you want to go back to living strictly by the law? Haven't you ever listened to what the law really says? Have you forgotten that Abraham had two sons; one by the slave girl, and the other by the freewoman?[b]

[23]*Ishmael*, the son of the slave girl, was born of the natural realm. But *Isaac*, the son of the freewoman, was born *supernaturally by the Spirit*—a child of the promise of God! [24]These two women and their sons express an allegory and become symbols of two covenants. The first covenant was born on Mount Sinai, birthing children into slavery—children born to Hagar. [25]For "Hagar" represents the law given at Mount Sinai in Arabia. *The "Hagar"*

---

a 4:17 Or "whispering enemies."
b 4:21–22 See Gen. 16:15; 21:2.

metaphor corresponds to the earthly Jerusalem of today who are currently in bondage.

[26]In contrast, there is a heavenly Jerusalem above us, which is our true "mother." She is the freewoman, birthing children into freedom![a] [27]For it is written:

"Burst forth with gladness,
    rejoice, O barren woman with no children,
break through with the shouts of joy and jubilee,
    for you are about to give birth!
The one who was once considered desolate and barren
    now has more children than the one who has a
        husband!"[b]

[28]Dear friends,[c] just like Isaac, we're now the true children who inherit the kingdom promises.[d] [29]And just as the son of the natural world at that time harassed the son born of the power of the Holy Spirit, so it is today. [30]And what does the Scripture tell us to do?

"Expel the slave mother with her son![e]
The son of the slave woman will not be a true heir—
    for the true heir of the promises is the son of the
        freewoman."[f]

---

a 4:26 Paul is showing that the law is a system of works that brings bondage and that the promise is a system of grace that brings true freedom.

b 4:27 See Isa. 54:1.

c 4:28 Or "brothers."

d 4:28 Or "royal proclamation."

e 4:30 See Gen. 21:10. This is showing that the two "sons" are not meant to live together. You cannot mingle law and grace, for only grace is based upon the promise of new life.

f 4:30 See Gen. 21:10–12; John 8:35.

³¹It's now so obvious! We're not the children of the slave woman; we're the supernatural sons of the freewoman—*sons of grace!*

A Life of Freedom

5 At last we have freedom, for Christ has set us free! We must always cherish this truth*ᵃ* and firmly refuse to go back into the bondage of our past.

²I, Paul, tell you: If you think there is benefit in circumcision and Jewish regulations, then you're acting as though Christ is not enough. ³I say it again emphatically: If you let yourselves be circumcised you are obliged to fulfill every single one of the commandments and regulations of the law!

⁴If you want to be made right with God by fulfilling the obligations of the law, you have cut off *more than your flesh*—you have cut yourselves off from Christ and have fallen away from *the revelation of* grace!

⁵But we have the true hope that comes from being made right with God, and by the Spirit we wait eagerly for this hope. ⁶When you're joined to the Anointed One, circumcision and religious obligations can benefit you nothing. All that matters now is living in the faith that works and expresses itself through love.

⁷Before you were led astray, you were so faithful.*ᵇ* Who has deceived you so that you have turned from what is right?

⁸The One who enfolded you into his grace is not behind this false teaching that you've embraced. ⁹Don't you know that when you allow even a little lie into your heart, it can permeate your entire belief system?*ᶜ*

---

a 5:1 Or "stand strong."
b 5:7 Or "you were running well."
c 5:9 Literally "A little yeast goes through the whole lump of dough." The text uses a metaphor of "yeast" that has effects that cannot be hidden when it is folded into dough. The yeast is the lie of legalism.

¹⁰Deep in my heart I have confidence that the Lord, who lives in you, will bring you back around to the truth. And I'm convinced that those who trouble you, whoever they think they are, will bear the penalty!

¹¹Dear friends, why do you think the religious system persecutes me? Is it because I preach the message of being circumcised and keeping all the laws of Judaism? Not at all! Is there no longer any offense over the cross? ¹²To tell you the truth, I am so disgusted with all your agitators. I wish they would go even further and cut off their legalistic influence from your lives!ᵃ

¹³Beloved ones, God has called us to live a life of freedom. But don't view this wonderful freedom as an excuse to set up a base of operations in the natural realm. Constantly love each other and be committed to serve one another.

¹⁴For all the law can be summarized in one grand statement:

"Demonstrate love to your neighbor, even as you
care for and love yourself."ᵇ

¹⁵But if you continue to criticize and come against each other over minor issues, you're acting like wild beasts trying to destroy one another!ᶜ

The Holy Spirit, Our Victory
¹⁶Let me emphasize this: As you yield to the dynamic life and power of the Holy Spirit, you will abandon the

---

a 5:12 Or "castrate themselves."

b 5:14 See Lev. 19:18.

c 5:15 Both Aramaic and Greek manuscripts read "biting and devouring," which is a metaphor for critical attitudes that will destroy the fellowship. These terms were often found in classical Greek literature to describe wild animals fighting each other in deadly conflict.

cravings of your self-life.[a] [17]When your self-life craves the things that offend the Holy Spirit *you hinder him from living free within you!* And the Holy Spirit's intense cravings hinder your self-life from dominating you! So then, the two incompatible and conflicting forces within you are your self-life of the flesh and the new creation life of the Spirit.[b]

[18]But when you yield to the life of the Spirit,[c] you will no longer be living under the law, *but soaring above it!*

[19]The behavior of the self-life is obvious: Sexual immorality, lustful thoughts, pornography, [20]chasing after things instead of God,[d] manipulating others,[e] hatred of those who get in your way, senseless arguments, resentment when others are favored, temper tantrums, angry quarrels, only thinking of yourself, being in love with your own opinions, [21]being envious of the blessings of others, murder, uncontrolled addictions,[f] wild parties, and all other similar behavior.

Haven't I already warned you that those who use their "freedom" for these things will not inherit the kingdom realm of God!

[22-23]But the fruit[g] produced by the Holy Spirit within you is divine love *in all its varied expressions:*[h]

---

a 5:16 Or "the natural realm."

b 5:17 The concept of the "new creation life of the Spirit" is implied in the greater context of Galatians, and referred to explicitly in 6:15–16.

c 5:18 The word for Spirit is actually "Spirit-Wind."

d 5:20 Literally "idolatry."

e 5:20 Literally "witchcraft." The Greek word for "witchcraft" can imply drug usage.

f 5:21 Literally "drunken binges."

g 5:22–23 The Greek word here can be translated "harvest."

h 5:22–23 There is clear textual inference that the "fruit" (singular) of the Holy Spirit is love, with the other virtues displaying aspects of the greatest quality of Spirit-life, *agape* love.

joy *that overflows,*[a]
peace *that subdues,*
patience[b] *that endures,*
kindness[c] *in action,*
a life full of virtue,[d]
faith *that prevails,*
gentleness *of heart,* and
strength *of spirit.*[e]

Never set the law above these qualities, for they are meant to be limitless.[f]

[24]Keep in mind that we who belong to Jesus Christ have already experienced crucifixion. For everything connected with our self-life[g] was put to death on the cross and crucified with Messiah. [25]If the Spirit is the source of our life, we must also allow the Spirit to direct every aspect of our lives. [26]So may we never be arrogant, or look down on another, *for each of us is an original.* We must forsake all jealousy that diminishes the value of others.[h]

Carry Each Other's Burdens

6 My beloved friends, if you see a believer who is overtaken with a fault,[i] the one who is in the Spirit should

---

a 5:22–23 This translation has chosen to supply action to these virtues, for they are not meant to be abstract virtues, but made visible with actions.

b 5:22–23 The Greek word for patience is taken from a verb that means "ever tapping" or "never quitting."

c 5:22–23 The Aramaic word can be translated "sweetness."

d 5:22–23 Or "goodness."

e 5:22–23 The word *self* is not found in this verse; however, most translations render this as "self-control." The word is actually "lordship," or by implication "spirit-strength."

f 5:22–23 Literally "there is no law set against these things" or "there is no conflict with Jewish laws."

g 5:24 Or "all our fleshly passions and desires." See 1 John 2:15–17.

h 5:26 As translated from the Aramaic.

i 6:1 Or "mistake."

seek to restore him in the Spirit of gentleness. But keep watch over your own heart so that you won't be tempted to exalt yourself over him.[a] [2]*Love empowers us to* fulfill the law of the Anointed One as we carry each other's troubles. [3]If you think you are somebody too important to stoop down to help another (when really you are not), you are living in deception.

[4]Let everyone be devoted to fulfill the work God has given them to do with excellence, and their joy will be in doing what's right and being themselves, and not in *being affirmed by* others. [5]Every believer is ultimately responsible for his or her own conscience.[b] [6]And those who are taught the Word must share all good things with their teacher.

We Harvest What We Plant

[7]God will never be mocked! For what you plant will always be the very thing you harvest. [8]*The harvest you reap reveals the seed that you planted.* If you plant the corrupt seeds of self-life into this natural realm, you can expect a harvest of corruption. If you plant the good seeds[c] of Spirit-life you will reap *beautiful fruits that grow* from the everlasting life of the Spirit.

[9]And don't allow yourselves to be weary in planting good seeds, for the season of reaping the wonderful harvest you've planted is coming! [10]Take advantage of every opportunity to be a blessing to others,[d] especially to our brothers and sisters in the family of faith!

---

a 6:1 Or "keep you from being harassed by the enemy."

b 6:5 As translated from the Aramaic.

c 6:8 These "good seeds" would include prayer, Bible study, speaking wise words, giving, loving, and dropping "seeds" of love and truth every day from our new creation life.

d 6:10 The Greek text implies giving finances.

Summary and Conclusion

[11]I've written this letter to you with my own handwriting—see how large I have to make the letters?[a] [12]All those who insist that you be circumcised are recruiting you so they can boast in their own achievement. They seek to avoid the persecution that comes with preaching the liberating message of the cross of Messiah! [13]Not even those who are circumcised keep every detail of the written law. Yet they push you to be circumcised so that they can boast that you have become like them.[b]

[14]May my only boast be found in the cross of our Lord Jesus Christ. In him I have been crucified to this natural realm;[c] and the natural realm is dead to me *and no longer dominates my life.*

[15]Whether a man is circumcised or uncircumcised is meaningless to me. What really matters is the transforming power of this new creation life. [16]And all those who live in agreement with this standard will have true peace and God's delight, for they are the Israel of God.[d]

[17]From now on, let no one cause me to suffer further, for I am carrying the very scars[e] of our Lord Jesus in my body. [18]Finally my beloved ones—may the wonderful grace of our Lord Jesus, the Anointed One, be flowing in your spirit.[f] So shall it be!

In Messiah's love,
Paul

---

a 6:11 Evidently, Paul had to write using large letters due to an eye problem (ch. 4:15). Some Greek texts imply that only beginning with v. 11 does Paul write in his own handwriting. The Aramaic indicates the entire letter was written in his handwriting.

b 6:13 Or "so that they can boast about your flesh."

c 6:14 Or "the world."

d 6:16 See ch. 3:7, 9, 29; Rom. 2:29; 4:12; 9:6–8; Phil. 3:3.

e 6:17 The Aramaic word for "scars" can also mean "death marks" or "stigmata."

f 6:18 Or "with your spirits." See 2 Tim. 4:22.

EPHESIANS

Introduction

AT A GLANCE

Author: The apostle Paul

Audience: The church of Ephesus, and surrounding area churches

Date: AD 60–62

Type of Literature: A letter

Major Themes: Salvation and grace, God's power, church unity, and Christian conduct and identity

Outline:

Letter Opening — 1:1–2

The Church's Heavenly Calling — 1:3–3:21

The Church's Earthly Conduct — 4:1–6:20

Letter Closing — 6:21–24

ABOUT EPHESIANS

What you are about to read is meant to be taught to every church. It is the constitution of our faith, the great summary description of all that is precious and esteemed in Christian doctrine and Christian living. Paul firmly plants the cornerstone of our faith in this powerful letter, cementing, in its few pages, the position and authority of the church over every other force. In it, Paul brings before every believer the mystery of the glory of Christ.

The theme of Ephesians is that God will one day submit everything under the leadership of Jesus Christ. He is the Head of the church and the fullness of God in human flesh. He gives his church extraordinary power to walk filled with the Holy Spirit, revealing the nature of God in all things. Jesus loves the church and cherishes everything about her. He is the one who brings Jews and non-Jews into one body. The church is God's new humanity—one new man. It is the new temple where God's glory dwells. And the church is the bride of Christ, the beloved partner who is destined to rule with him.

How wonderfully he blesses his bride with gifts from above. He gives us, both men and women, the grace to be apostles, prophets, evangelists, pastors, and teachers who will feed and encourage the church to rise higher. The greatness of God streams from Jesus Christ into the hearts of every believer. These are the grand themes of Ephesians.

I have always loved the apostolic prayers of Paul, especially those found in Ephesians. I have prayed nearly every day for forty years that God would impart to me the spirit of revelation and the spirit of wisdom to guide my life, my family, and my ministry. God is good to give the Holy Spirit's fullness to those who ask with sincere hunger for more.

PURPOSE

What an exciting letter Paul has written to us! Ephesians is full of life and its words reach higher in Christian thought than any letter in our New Testament. Full of living revelation, it simply drips with the anointing of the Holy Spirit. Where most of Paul's letters are addressed to churches facing specific issues dealing with belief and practice, this isn't the case with Ephesians. There is a more general, theologically reflective tone to this letter that is meant to ground, shape, and challenge believers (mainly gentile) in their faith.

AUTHOR AND AUDIENCE

Paul wrote this letter about AD 60, while in a prison cell in Rome, and sent it with Tychicus as a circular letter that was to be read to all the churches.

Originally, there were no titles on Paul's letters. They were gathered and the titles were assigned according to where they were sent; then they were published for the churches as a group. In none of the earliest Greek manuscripts did the words *Ephesus* or *Ephesians* occur. It was simply added in the margin next to the main text in the first copies made. The conclusion by some scholars is that this letter to the Ephesians may possibly be the lost letter of the Laodiceans mentioned in Col. 4:16: "Once you've read this letter publicly to the church, please send it on to the church of the Laodiceans, and make sure you read the letter that I wrote to them." Others believe it was intended for Ephesus as it stands today.

Scholars are not sure on this point; it is the only letter Paul wrote that did not contain any personal greetings to specific people. Since these greetings easily identified the other letters, many now believe this letter was written not only for the Ephesians but for Christians in the surrounding area too.

MAJOR THEMES

Salvation by Grace through Faith. Paul paints a very bleak picture of who we were before God stepped in to rescue us: "you were once like corpses, dead in your sins and offenses" (2:1). Yet he goes on: "Even when we were dead and doomed in our many sins, he united us into the very life of Christ and saved us by his wonderful grace!" (2:5). Paul makes it clear we don't earn or work for this rescue; rather, it's God's undeserved favor from beginning to end!

Power of God over All Others. One of the leading themes in this letter from heaven is the theme that God's power trumps that of all other principalities, powers, and authorities in this world. For Paul, any threat of the spiritual powers of this world should be seen in light of the superior power of God and the power we have as his children.

Christian Unity. Another leading theme in Paul's letter is the unity that Jews and non-Jews share in Christ. Paul's strong encouragement for unity and love within the body work together to encourage believers to overcome any and all cultural pressures of animosity on the basis of Jesus' work uniting all believers into one community of people.

Christian Conduct. Most of chs. 3–6 focus on how Christians should live, especially new believers, which is summed up with Paul's appeal in 4:17 to "not live like the unbelievers around you who walk in their empty delusions." Paul urges new believers—and really all believers—to cultivate a lifestyle consistent with their new life in Christ—a life free from drunkenness, sexual immorality, lying, stealing, bitterness, and other ungodly behaviors.

Christian Identity. One of the major themes of Paul's teachings is the fact that believers are now "in Christ," an idea that impacts every aspect of believers' identity. We exist in a personal, energizing relationship of unity with the risen Christ! This identity is crucial in our ongoing struggle with spiritual darkness and powers, maintaining Christian unity, overcoming our former lifestyle, and living as God has called us to live.

EPHESIANS

Heaven's Riches

Paul's Introduction

1 *Dear friends,*

My name is Paul, and I was chosen by God to be an apostle of Jesus, the Messiah. [2]I'm writing this letter to all the devoted believers[a] who have been made holy[b] by being one with Jesus, the Anointed One.

May God himself, the heavenly Father of our Lord Jesus Christ, release grace over you and impart total well-being[c] into your lives.

Our Sonship and the Father's Plan

[3]Every spiritual blessing in the heavenly realm has already been lavished upon us as a love gift from our wonderful heavenly Father, the Father of our Lord Jesus—all

---

a 1:2 Recent manuscripts add the words "those who are in Ephesus." The oldest manuscripts have "to the Ephesians" written in the margin. This would reinforce the theory that it is meant to be read and distributed to all the churches. Although the book bears the name "Ephesians," some scholars believe that this letter could be the missing letter to the Laodiceans mentioned in Col. 4:16. Regardless, Ephesians contains crucial truths for believers worldwide.

b 1:2 Or "to the saints [holy ones] and the faithful in Christ Jesus." Notice that God is the one who makes us holy, but our response is to be "faithful" (or "devoted").

c 1:2 Or "peace." The Hebrew concept of peace means much more than tranquility.

because he sees us wrapped into Christ. This is why we celebrate him[a] with all our hearts!

[4]And in love he chose us before he laid the foundation of the universe![b] Because of his great love, he ordained us, so that we would be seen as holy in his eyes with an unstained innocence.

[5-6]For it was always in his perfect plan[c] to adopt[d] us as his delightful children, through our union with Jesus, the Anointed One, so that his tremendous love that cascades over us would glorify his grace[e]—for the same love he has for the Beloved, Jesus, he has for us. And this unfolding plan brings him great pleasure!

[7]Since we are now joined to Christ, we have been given the treasures of redemption by his blood—the total cancellation[f] of our sins—all because of the cascading riches[g] of his grace. [8]This *superabundant* grace is already powerfully working in us,[h] releasing all forms of wisdom and practical understanding. [9]And through the revelation of the Anointed One, he unveiled his secret desires

---

a 1:3 Or "bless" (or "blessed be God").

b 1:4 There is an alternate Greek translation of the unique wording of this verse that could be translated "He chose us to be a 'word' before the fall of the world." The Greek word for "chose" is *eklego-mai*, which is a form of *lego* (speak). The word for "fall" (Adam's fall) is *kataboles*, which can mean "falling down," but is usually translated as "foundation" (of the world).

c 1:5–6 Or "He marked out our horizon [destiny] beforehand."

d 1:5–6 The Aramaic reads "to establish us."

e 1:5–6 Or "to praise upon praise of the glory of his grace."

f 1:7 Or "forgiveness." The Greek word *aphesis* means "to send away" or "to set free" (from bondage).

g 1:7 The Greek word for "riches" (*ploutos*) is also used to describe God's wisdom and knowledge in Rom. 11:33. Just as God is all-knowing and has all-wisdom, so he has untold riches of grace available for his children.

h 1:8 Or "lavished on us."

to us—the hidden mystery of his long-range plan, which he was delighted to implement from the very beginning of time. [10]And because of God's unfailing purpose, this detailed plan will reign supreme through every period of time until the fulfillment of all the ages finally reaches its climax—when God makes all things new[a] in all of heaven and earth through Jesus Christ.

[11]Through our union with Christ we too have been claimed by God as his own inheritance.[b] Before we were even born, he gave us our destiny;[c] that we would fulfill the plan of God who always accomplishes every purpose and plan in his heart. [12]God's purpose was that we *Jews*, who were the first to long for the messianic hope, would be the first to believe in the Anointed One and bring great praise and glory to God!

[13]And because of him, when you *who are not Jews* heard the revelation[d] of truth, you believed in the wonderful news of salvation. Now we have been stamped with the seal of the promised Holy Spirit.[e]

[14]He is given to us like an engagement ring,[f] as the first installment of what's coming! He is our hope-promise of a future inheritance[g] which seals us until we have

---

a 1:10 As translated from the Aramaic. The Greek text states "God will gather together all things in fulfillment in Christ." That is, God will unite all things under the headship of Christ.

b 1:11 The Greek construction of this phrase can mean either that God appointed us (Gr. *klēroō*, chosen by casting lots) to be his inheritance, or that we have been appointed an inheritance.

c 1:11 Or "estate."

d 1:13 The Greek text is *logos* or "word of God."

e 1:13 Some Aramaic manuscripts add here "who was announced by the angels."

f 1:14 The Greek word used here can be translated "pledge," "down payment" or "engagement ring."

g 1:14 The Aramaic word used for "inheritance" can also be translated "dividend."

all of redemption's promises and experience complete freedom—all for the supreme glory and honor of God!

Paul Prays for the Spirit of Wisdom and Revelation

[15]Because of this, since I first heard about your strong faith in the Lord Jesus Christ and your tender love toward all his devoted ones, [16]my heart is always full and overflowing with thanks to God for you as I constantly remember you in my prayers.[a] [17]I pray that the Father of glory, the God of our Lord Jesus Christ, would impart to you the riches of the Spirit of wisdom and the Spirit of revelation[b] to know him through your deepening intimacy with him.

[18]I pray that the light of God will illuminate the eyes of your imagination,[c] flooding you with light, until you experience the full revelation of the hope of his calling[d]—that is, the wealth of God's glorious inheritances that he finds in us, his holy ones!

[19]I pray that you will continually experience the immeasurable greatness of God's power made available to you through faith. Then your lives will be an advertisement of this immense power as it works through you! This is the mighty power [20]that was released when God raised Christ from the dead and exalted him[e] to the place of highest honor and supreme authority[f] in the heavenly realm! [21]And now he is exalted as first above every ruler, authority, government, and realm of power in existence! He is gloriously enthroned over every name that is ever

---

a 1:16 The literal Aramaic text can be translated "I began confessing on your behalf and praying."

b 1:17 Or "discovery."

c 1:18 Or "innermost" (heart).

d 1:18 Or "to which he is calling you."

e 1:20 Or "he seated him" (enthroned).

f 1:20 Or "at his right hand," a metaphor for the place of honor and authority.

praised,[a] not only in this age,[b] but in the age that is coming![c]

[22]And he alone is the leader and source of everything needed in the church. God has put everything beneath the authority of Jesus Christ[d] *and has given him the highest rank above all others.* [23]And now we, his church, are his body on the earth and that which fills him who is being filled by it![e]

God's Power Raised Us from the Dead

2 *And his fullness fills you,* even though you were once like corpses,[f] dead in your sins and offenses. [2]It wasn't that long ago that you lived in the religion, customs, and values[g] of this world,[h] obeying the dark ruler of the earthly realm who fills the atmosphere with his authority, and works diligently in the hearts of those who are disobedient to the truth of God. [3]The corruption that was in us from birth was expressed through the deeds and desires of our self-life. We lived by whatever natural cravings and thoughts our minds dictated, living as rebellious children subject to God's wrath like everyone else.

[4]But God still loved us with such great love. He is so rich in compassion and mercy. [5]Even when we were dead

---

a 1:21 As translated from the Aramaic.

b 1:21 The Aramaic word can be translated "universe."

c 1:21 As translated from the Aramaic.

d 1:22 Both Greek and Aramaic texts use the figure of speech "under his feet," which means he has conquered, subdued, and now rules over them.

e 1:23 That is, as we are those who are filled (completed) by Christ, we also complete (fill) him. What a wonderful and humbling mystery is revealed by this verse.

f 2:1 As translated literally from the Greek.

g 2:2 The Aramaic can be translated "the worldliness of this world."

h 2:2 The Aramaic phrase can also refer to the authority of secular governments.

and doomed in our many sins, he united us into the very life of Christ and saved us by his wonderful grace! ⁶He raised us up with Christ the exalted One, *and we ascended with him into the glorious perfection and authority* of the heavenly realm, for we are now co-seated*ᵃ* as one with Christ!

⁷Throughout the coming ages*ᵇ* we will be the visible display of the infinite riches of his grace and kindness, which was showered upon us in Jesus Christ. ⁸For by grace you have been saved by faith. Nothing you did could ever earn this salvation, for it was the love gift*ᶜ* from God that brought us to Christ! ⁹So no one will ever be able to boast, for salvation is never a reward for good works or human striving.

¹⁰We have become his poetry,*ᵈ* a re-created people that will fulfill the destiny he has given each of us, for we are joined to Jesus, the Anointed One. Even before we were born, God planned in advance *our destiny* and the good works*ᵉ* we would do *to fulfill it!*

A New Humanity

¹¹⁻¹²So don't forget that you were not born as Jews and were uncircumcised (circumcision itself is just a work of man's hands); you had none of the Jewish covenants and

---

a 2:6 To be "placed" or "seated" in heaven means we have been given the perfection and authority to be there.

b 2:7 The Aramaic can be translated "universes."

c 2:8 The Aramaic word for "gift" is *mohabata* and comes from the Aramaic word *chav,* which means "love."

d 2:10 The beautiful Greek word used here is translated "poem" or "poetry." Our lives are the beautiful poetry written by God that will speak forth all that he desires in life.

e 2:10 Although implied, these good works make up our destiny. As we yield to God, our prearranged destiny comes to pass and we are rewarded for simply doing what he wanted us to accomplish.

laws; you were foreigners to Israel's incredible heritage;[a] you were without the covenants and prophetic promises of the Messiah, the promised hope, and without God.

[13]*Yet look at you now! Everything is new!* Although you were once distant and far away from God, now you have been brought delightfully close to him through the sacred blood of Jesus—you have actually been united to Christ!

[14]Our reconciling "Peace" is Jesus! He has made Jew and non-Jew one *in Christ. By dying as our sacrifice*, he has broken down every wall of prejudice that separated us *and has now made us equal through our union with Christ.* [15]Ethnic hatred has been dissolved by the crucifixion of his precious body on the cross. The legal code that stood condemning every one of us has now been repealed *by his command.* His triune essence has made peace between us by starting over—forming[b] one new race of humanity,[c] Jews and non-Jews fused together in himself!

[16]Two have now become one, and we live restored to God and reconciled in the body of Christ. Through his crucifixion, hatred died. [17]For the Messiah has come to preach this sweet message of peace to you,[d] the ones who were distant, and to those who are near. [18]And now, because we are united to Christ, we both have equal and direct access in the realm of the Holy Spirit to come before the Father!

[19]So, you are not foreigners or guests, but rather you are the children of the city of the holy ones,[e] with all the rights as family members of the household of God. [20]*You*

---

a 2:11–12 Or "freedom," or "commonwealth."

b 2:15 As translated from the Aramaic. The Greek is "to create in himself one new man."

c 2:15 Or "one new man."

d 2:17 This is Paul's paraphrase of Isa. 57:19.

e 2:19 As translated from the Aramaic.

are rising like the perfectly fitted stones of the temple;^a and your lives have been built up together upon the foundation laid by the apostles and prophets, and best of all, you are connected to the Head Cornerstone of the building, the Anointed One, Jesus Christ himself!

²¹This entire building is under construction and is continually growing under his supervision until it rises up completed as the holy temple of the Lord himself. ²²This means that God is transforming each one of you into *the Holy of Holies*, his dwelling place, through the power of the Holy Spirit living in you!

The Divine Mystery

3 Beloved friends, *because of my love for Jesus Christ*, I am now his prisoner for the sake of all of you who are not Jews, ²so that you will hear the gospel that God has entrusted to me to share with you. ³For this wonderful mystery, which I briefly described, was given to me by divine revelation, ⁴so that whenever you read it you will be able to understand my revelation and insight into the secret mystery of the Messiah.

⁵There has never been a generation that has been given the detailed understanding of this glorious and divine mystery until now. He kept it a secret until this generation. God is revealing it only now to his sacred apostles and prophets by the Holy Spirit. ⁶Here's the secret: The gospel of grace has made you, non-Jewish believers, into coheirs of his promise through your union with him. And you have now become members of his body—one with the Anointed One!

⁷⁻⁸I have been made a messenger of this wonderful news by the gift of grace that works through me. Even though

---

a 2:20 The "temple" is not found in the text here, but is explicitly mentioned in v. 21.

I am the least significant of all his holy believers, this grace-gift was imparted when the manifestation of his power came upon me. Grace alone empowers me so that I can boldly preach this wonderful message to non-Jewish people, sharing with them the unfading,[a] inexhaustible riches of Christ, which are beyond comprehension.

[9]My passion is to enlighten every person to this divine mystery. It was hidden for ages past until now, and kept a secret in the heart of God, the Creator of all. [10]The purpose of this was to unveil before every throne and rank of angelic orders in the heavenly realm God's full and diverse wisdom revealed through the church.[b] [11]This perfectly wise plan was destined from eternal ages and fulfilled completely in our Lord Jesus Christ, so that now [12]we have boldness through him,[c] and free access as kings[d] before the Father because of our complete confidence in Christ's faithfulness.

[13]My dear friends, I pray that you will remain strong and not be discouraged or ashamed by all that I suffer on your behalf, for it is for your glory.

Paul Prays for Love to Overflow
[14]So I kneel humbly in awe before the Father of our Lord Jesus, the Messiah, [15]the perfect Father of every father

---

a 3:7–8 The word *unfading* comes from an Aramaic word which can also be translated "unquestionable" or "without fault." The Greek uses the word *unsearchable*.

b 3:10 The church is the "university of the angels" and every believer is a "professor" teaching the heavenly realm the mysteries and wonders of the grace of God. The angels investigate through our lives the treasures of grace, like the cherubim who gaze upon the mercy seat. See 1 Peter 1:12.

c 3:12 The Greek words used here can be translated, "freedom of speech to say whatever you want with boldness."

d 3:12 The Aramaic text can be translated "we have kingship."

and child*ᵃ* in heaven and on the earth. ¹⁶And I pray that he would unveil within you the unlimited riches of his glory and favor until supernatural strength floods your innermost being with his divine might and explosive power.

¹⁷Then, by constantly using your faith, the life of Christ will be released deep inside you, and the resting place of his love will become the very source and root of your life.

¹⁸⁻¹⁹Then you will be empowered to discover what every holy one experiences—the great magnitude*ᵇ* of the astonishing love of Christ in all its dimensions. How deeply intimate and far-reaching is his love! How enduring and inclusive it is! Endless love beyond measurement that transcends our understanding—this extravagant love pours into you until you are filled to overflowing with the fullness of God!

²⁰*Never doubt* God's mighty power to work in you and accomplish all this. He will achieve infinitely more than your greatest request, your most unbelievable dream, and exceed your wildest imagination!*ᶜ* He will outdo them all, for his miraculous power constantly energizes you.

²¹Now we offer up to God all the glorious praise that rises from every church in every generation through Jesus Christ—and all that will yet be manifest through time and eternity. Amen!

---

a 3:15 Translated from the Aramaic. It could also be translated "the perfect Father of every people group." The Greek word for "father" and the word for "family" are quite similar, which indicates that every family finds its source in the Father.

b 3:18–19 Or "excellence."

c 3:20 See 1 Kings 10:13.

Our Divine Calling

4 As a prisoner of the Lord,[a] I plead with you to walk holy, in a way that is suitable to your high rank, given to you in your divine calling. [2]With tender humility and quiet patience, always demonstrate gentleness and generous[b] love toward one another, especially toward those who may try your patience. [3]Be faithful to guard the sweet harmony of the Holy Spirit among you in the bonds of peace, [4]being one body and one spirit, as you were all called into the same glorious hope *of divine destiny.*

[5]For the Lord God is one, *and so are we,* for we share in one faith, one baptism, and one Father. [6]And he is the perfect Father who leads us all, works through us all, and lives in us all!

The Grace-Gifts of Christ

[7]And he has generously given each one of us supernatural grace, according to the size of the gift of Christ. [8]This is why he says:

"He ascends into the heavenly heights
    taking his many captured ones with him,[c]
    and gifts were given to men."[d]

[9]He "ascended" means that he returned to heaven, after he had first descended from the heights of heaven, even to the lower regions, namely, the earth. [10]The same one who descended is also the one who ascended above the

---

a 4:1 Paul wrote this letter while a prisoner in Rome because of his faith in Christ. See Song. 8:6.

b 4:2 The Aramaic word literally means "stretching."

c 4:8 Or "he captured captivity."

d 4:8 Or "men were given as gifts." See Ps. 68:18.

heights of heaven, in order to begin the restoration and fulfillment[a] of all things.

[11]And he has appointed some *with grace* to be apostles, and some *with grace* to be prophets, and some *with grace* to be evangelists,[b] and some *with grace* to be pastors,[c] and some *with grace* to be teachers.[d] [12]And their calling is to nurture and prepare all the holy believers to do their own works of ministry, and as they do this they will enlarge and build up the body of Christ. [13]*These grace ministries will function* until we all attain oneness into the faith, until we all experience the fullness of what it means to know the Son of God,[e] and finally we become one into a perfect man[f] with the full dimensions of spiritual maturity and fully developed into the abundance of Christ.

[14]And then our immaturity will end! And we will not be easily shaken by trouble, nor led astray by novel teachings or by the false doctrines of deceivers[g] who teach clever lies. [15]But instead we will remain strong and always sincere in our love as we express the truth. *All our direction and ministries will flow* from Christ and lead us deeper into him, the anointed Head of his body, the church.

---

a 4:10 As translated from the Aramaic. The Greek text says "that he might fill all things."

b 4:11 The Aramaic can be translated "preachers."

c 4:11 Or "shepherds."

d 4:11 The Aramaic can be translated "wise orators."

e 4:13 The Greek literally means "until we have the full knowledge of the Son of God."

f 4:13 The Hebrew and Aramaic word for "perfect" is *gamar*, and the word implies that perfection cannot come to the body of Christ without the example and teaching of these five ministries—apostles, prophets, evangelists, pastors, and teachers. To ignore these five ministry gifts of the ascended Christ for today is to despise the gifts that God has given to the church.

g 4:14 The Greek literally means "dice-playing gamblers."

¹⁶For his "body" *has been formed in his image* and is closely joined together and constantly connected as one. And every member *has been given divine gifts* to contribute to the growth of all; and as *these gifts* operate effectively throughout the whole body, we are built up and made perfect in love.

Our New Life in Christ

¹⁷So with the wisdom given to me from the Lord I say: You should not live like the unbelievers around you who walk in their empty delusions.ᵃ ¹⁸Their corrupted logic has been clouded because their hearts are so far from God—their blinded understanding and deep-seated moral darkness keeps them from the true knowledge of God. ¹⁹Because of spiritual apathy, they surrender their lives to lewdness, impurity, and sexual obsession.

²⁰But this is not the way of life that Christ has unfolded within you. ²¹If you have really experienced the Anointed One, and heard his truth, *it will be seen in your life*; for we know that the ultimate realityᵇ is embodied in Jesus!

²²And he has taught you to let go of the lifestyle of the ancient man,ᶜ the old self-life, which was corrupted by sinful and deceitful desires that spring from delusions. ²³Now it's time to be made new by every revelation that's been given to you.ᵈ ²⁴And to be transformed as you embrace the glorious Christ-within as your new life and live in union with him! For God has re-created you all over again in his perfect righteousness, and you now belong to him in the realm of true holiness. ²⁵So discard every form of dishonesty and lying *so that you will*

---

a 4:17 Or "opinions."
b 4:21 Or "ultimate learning."
c 4:22 As translated from the Aramaic.
d 4:23 Or "in the spirit of your revelation."

be known as one who always speaks the truth, for we all belong to one another.

[26]But don't let the passion of your emotions[a] lead you to sin! Don't let anger control you *or be fuel for revenge*, not for even a day. [27]Don't give the slanderous accuser, the Devil, an opportunity to manipulate you! [28]If any one of you has stolen from someone else, never do it again. Instead, be industrious, earning an honest living, and then you'll have enough to bless those in need.

[29]And never let ugly or hateful words come from your mouth, but instead let your words become beautiful gifts[b] that encourage others; do this by speaking words of grace to help them.

[30]The Holy Spirit of God has sealed you in Jesus Christ until you experience your full salvation. So never grieve the Spirit of God or take for granted his holy influence in your life.[c] [31]Lay aside bitter words, temper tantrums, revenge, profanity, and insults. [32]But instead be kind[d] and affectionate toward one another. Has God graciously forgiven you? Then graciously forgive one another in the depths of Christ's love.

Living in God's Love

5 Be imitators of God in everything you do,[e] for then you will represent your Father as his beloved sons

---

a 4:26 The Aramaic word *ragza* means "to shake" or "to tremble." It is a word used for any strong emotion, but usually refers to anger.

b 4:29 Or "constructive."

c 4:30 The Greek manuscripts have "do not grieve," while the Aramaic text reads "do not limit his scope." This translation includes both concepts.

d 4:32 The Aramaic word for "kind" can also be translated "sweet."

e 5:1 The Greek word *mimetes* frequently depicts an actor playing a role. God wants us to mimic him and be filled with his thoughts, his love, his deeds, and his character.

and daughters. [2]And continue to walk surrendered to the extravagant love of Christ, for he surrendered his life as a sacrifice for us. His great love for us was pleasing to God, like an aroma of adoration—a sweet healing fragrance.[a]

[3]And have nothing to do with sexual immorality, lust, or greed—for you are his holy ones *and let no one be able to accuse you of them in any form.* [4]Guard your speech. Forsake obscenities and worthless insults; these are non-sensical words that bring disgrace and are unnecessary. Instead, let worship fill your heart and spill out in your words.

[5]For it has been made clear to you already that the kingdom of God cannot be accessed by anyone who is guilty of sexual sin, or who is impure or greedy—for greed is the essence of idolatry. How could they expect to have an inheritance in Christ's kingdom *while doing those things*?

Living in God's Light

[6]Don't be fooled by those who speak their empty words and deceptive teachings telling you otherwise. This is what brings God's anger upon the rebellious! [7]Don't listen to them or live like them at all. [8]Once your life was full of sin's darkness, but now you have the very light of our Lord shining through you because of your union with him. Your mission is to live as children flooded with his revelation-light! [9]And the supernatural fruits of his light[b] will be seen in you—goodness, righteousness, and truth. [10]Then you will learn to choose what is beautiful to our Lord.

[11]And don't even associate with the servants of darkness because they have no fruit in them; instead, reveal truth

---

a 5:2 The Aramaic word for "fragrance" can also be translated "healing balm."

b 5:9 Some Greek manuscripts have "Spirit."

to them. ¹²The very things they do in secret are too vile and filthy to even mention. ¹³Whatever the revelation-light exposes, it will also correct, and everything that reveals truth is light to the soul.ᵃ ¹⁴This is why the Scripture says,

"Arise, you sleeper! Rise up from your coffin and the Anointed One will shine his light into you!"ᵇ

Living in God's Wisdom
¹⁵⁻¹⁶So be very careful how you live, not being like those with no understanding, but live honorably with true wisdom, for we are living in evil times. Take full advantage of every day as you spend your life for his purposes. ¹⁷And don't live foolishly for then you will have discernment to fully understand God's will. ¹⁸And don't get drunk with wine, which is rebellion;ᶜ instead be filled continually with the Holy Spirit.ᵈ ¹⁹*And your hearts will overflow with* a joyful song to the Lord. Keep speaking to each other with words of Scripture, singing the Psalms with praises and spontaneous songs given by the Spirit!ᵉ ²⁰Always give thanks to Father God for every personᶠ *he brings into your life* in the name of our Lord Jesus Christ.

---

a 5:13 Or "everything revealed becomes light."
b 5:14 See Isa. 26:19; 51:17; 52:1; 60:1.
c 5:18 The Aramaic can be translated "the wine of the prodigal." The Greek is "reckless living" or "debauchery."
d 5:18 Or "be inebriated in the Spirit's fullness."
e 5:19 Or "spiritual songs." There is no other song more spiritual than the Song of Songs. Perhaps Paul was encouraging the church to sing and rejoice in the greatest of all songs.
f 5:20 The Greek text is ambiguous; it can mean "give thanks for all things" or "for all people." The Aramaic is quite specific—"for all people."

Loving Relationships

[21]And out of your reverence for Christ be supportive of each other in love. [22]For wives, this means being devoted[a] to your husbands like you are tenderly devoted to our Lord, [23]for the husband provides leadership for the wife, just as Christ provides leadership for his church, as the Savior and Reviver[b] of the body. [24]In the same way the church is devoted to Christ, let the wives be devoted to their husbands in everything.

[25]And to the husbands, you are to demonstrate love for your wives with the same tender devotion that Christ demonstrated to us, his bride.[c] For he died for us, sacrificing himself [26]to make us holy and pure, cleansing us through the showering of the pure water of the Word of God. [27]*All that he does in us is designed* to make us a mature church for his pleasure, until we become a source of praise to him—glorious and radiant,[d] beautiful and holy, without fault or flaw.[e]

[28]Husbands have the obligation of loving and caring for their wives the same way they love and care for their own bodies, for to love your wife is to love your own self. [29]No one abuses his own body, but pampers it—serving and satisfying its needs. That's exactly what Christ does for his church! [30]*He serves and satisfies us[f]* as members of his body.

---

a 5:22 The Greek word for "submit," or "supportive," is not found in v. 22. It is literally "Wives, with your husbands."

b 5:23 The Aramaic word used here can be translated "Savior" or "Reviver." This translation includes both concepts.

c 5:25 Or "church."

d 5:27 The Greek word for "radiance" (*endoxos*) can also mean "gorgeous," "honorable," "esteemed," "splendid," "infused with glory." This is what Christ's love will do to you. (See *Strong's Concordance*, Gr. 1741.)

e 5:27 The Greek text has "without any wrinkle." The Aramaic can be translated "without chips or knots."

f 5:30 Inferred from v. 29 and made explicit here.

³¹For this reason a man is to leave his father and his mother and lovingly hold to his wife, since the two have become joined as one flesh.ᵃ ³²Marriage is the beautiful design of the Almighty,ᵇ a great mysteryᶜ of Christ and his church. ³³So every married man should be gracious to his wife just as he is gracious to himself. And every wife should be tenderly devoted to her husband.

Love in Our Families and Workplaces

6 Children, *if you want to be wise*, listen to your parents and do what they tell you, and the Lordᵈ will help you.

²For the commandment, "Honor your father and your mother," was the first of the *Ten Commandments* with a promise attached: ³"You will prosperᵉ and live a long, full life *if you honor your parents.*"

⁴Fathers, don't exasperate your children,ᶠ but raise them up with loving discipline and counsel that brings the revelation of our Lord.

⁵Those who are employed should listen to their employersᵍ and obey their instructions with great respect and honor.ʰ Serve them with humility in your hearts as though you were working for the Master.ⁱ

---

a 5:31 See Gen. 2:24.

b 5:32 As translated from the Aramaic.

c 5:32 Or "megamystery." No book of the Bible unveils more of this great megamystery than does the Song of Songs.

d 6:1 Or "through our Lord."

e 6:3 Or "it will go beautifully for you."

f 6:4 In other words, fathers should show consideration for the different levels of understanding and experience that children possess, dealing with them at their level, or risk causing them loads of heartache.

g 6:5 Literally "servants should obey their caretakers."

h 6:5 Or "with trembling."

i 6:5 Or "the Messiah."

⁶Always do what is right and not only when others are watching, so that you may please Christ as his servants by doing his will. ⁷Serve^a your employers wholeheartedly and with love, as though you were serving Christ and not men. ⁸Be assured that anything you do that is beautiful and excellent will be repaid by our Lord, whether you are an employee or an employer.

⁹And to the caretakers of the flock^b I say, do what is right with your people by forgiving them when they offend you, for you know there is a Master in heaven that shows no favoritism.

Spiritual Warfare

¹⁰Now my beloved ones, I have saved these most important truths for last: Be supernaturally infused with strength through your life-union with the Lord Jesus. Stand victorious with the force^c of his explosive power flowing in and through you.

¹¹Put on God's complete set of armor^d provided for us, so that you will be protected as you fight against the evil strategies of the accuser!^e ¹²Your hand-to-hand combat is not with human beings, but with the highest principalities and authorities operating in rebellion under the heavenly realms.^f For they are a powerful class of

---

a 6:7 Or "minister to them."
b 6:9 As translated literally from the Aramaic. The "caretakers of the flock" can refer to both leadership in the church and in the workplace. The Greek text states "masters, do the same things to them, and give up threatening."
c 6:10 Or "weapons."
d 6:11 See Isa. 59:17.
e 6:11 Or "the devil."
f 6:12 Or literally "under heaven."

demon-gods[a] and evil spirits that hold[b] this dark world in bondage. [13]Because of this, you must wear all the armor that God provides so you're protected as you confront the slanderer,[c] for you are destined for all things[d] and will rise victorious.

[14]Put on truth as a belt to strengthen you to stand in triumph. Put on holiness as the protective armor that covers your heart. [15]Stand on your feet alert, then you'll always be ready to share the blessings of peace.

[16]In every battle, take faith as your wrap-around shield, for it is able to extinguish the blazing arrows coming at you from the evil one![e] [17-18]Embrace the power of salvation's full deliverance, like a helmet *to protect your thoughts from lies*. And take the mighty razor-sharp Spirit-sword[f] of the spoken word of God.

Pray passionately[g] in the Spirit, as you constantly intercede with every form of prayer at all times. Pray the blessings of God upon all his believers. [19]And pray also that God's revelation would be released through me every time I preach the wonderful mystery of the *hope-filled* gospel. [20]Yes, pray that I may preach the wonderful news of God's kingdom with bold freedom at every opportunity. Even though I am chained as a prisoner, I am his ambassador.

---

a 6:12 The classical Greek word used here is often used to refer to conjuring up pagan deities—supreme powers of darkness mentioned in occult rituals.

b 6:12 Or "possessors of this dark world."

c 6:13 Or "devil."

d 6:13 As translated from the Aramaic. The Greek text can be translated "after you have conquered, you can stand in victory."

e 6:16 The poetic language Paul uses here is likely a reference to Ps. 91:4–5.

f 6:17–18 This is the Greek word *machaira*, which was a razor-sharp Roman sword used in close combat.

g 6:17–18 Or "all desires."

The Messenger, Tychicus

[21-22]I am sending you a dear friend, Tychicus.[a] He is a beloved brother and trustworthy minister in our Lord Jesus. He will share with you all the concerns that I have for your welfare and will inform you of how I am getting along. And he will also prophesy over you[b] to encourage your hearts. [23]So may God shower his peace upon you, my beloved friends. And may the blessings of faith and love fill your hearts from God the Father and from our Lord Jesus, the Messiah. [24]Abundant grace will be with you all as each of you love our Lord Jesus Christ without corruption. Amen!

Love in Christ,
Paul

---

a 6:21–22 Tychicus, whose name means "child of fortune," is believed to be an Ephesian who took this letter, as Paul's representative, to the churches throughout Turkey. He is mentioned four other times in the New Testament. See Acts 20:4; Col. 4:7; 2 Tim. 4:12; and Titus 3:12.

b 6:21–22 Translated from the Aramaic. Prophecy in the local church will always encourage, edify, and enlighten. See 1 Cor. 14:3.

PHILIPPIANS

Introduction

AT A GLANCE

Author: The apostle Paul
Audience: The church of Philippi
Date: AD 60–62
Type of Literature: A letter
Major Themes: The gospel of joy, Christ's lordship, Christian conduct, and Christ's community and identity
Outline:

Letter Opening — 1:1–11
Paul's Gospel Priority — 1:12–26
Gospel-Living Conduct — 1:27–2:18
Examples of Gospel-Living — 2:19–30
Paul's Gospel Experience — 3:1–21
Final Encouragements — 4:1–9
Letter Closing — 4:10–23

ABOUT PHILIPPIANS

What joy and glory came out of Paul's prison cell! Most of us would be thinking of ourselves and how we could get out; but Paul wanted to send to the Philippian church the revelation of joy!

The church of Philippi began because of a supernatural vision experienced by Paul while he was ministering at Troas (Acts 16:8–10). He had a vision in the night of a man from Macedonia who stood at his bedside pleading with him to come and give them the gospel.

It was in Philippi that Paul was arrested for preaching the gospel. Thrown in a prison cell and beaten, he and his coworker Silas began to sing songs of joy and praise to the Most High God! This caused a tremendous miracle as the prison doors were flung open and they escaped—but not before leading their jailor to Christ! Perhaps the jailor was the very man Paul had seen in his vision.

Philippi is where Paul met Lydia, a businesswoman who apparently led an import/export business from that city. The miracles of God birthed a church among the Philippians, and Paul longs to encourage them to never give up and to keep rejoicing in all things.

Paul's words point us to heaven. He teaches us that our true life is not only in this world, but it is in the heavenly calling, the heavenly realm, and in our heavenly life that was given to us through Christ, the heavenly Man. He left heaven to redeem us and reveal the heart of God, the heart of a servant. He gave us new birth that we would be heavenly lights in this dark world as witnesses of Christ's power to change our lives.

There is a good and glorious work that Christ has begun in our hearts and promises to complete once he is fully unveiled. Philippians teaches us how important it is to be joyful throughout our journey of becoming like Christ. The words *joy* and *rejoicing* occur eighteen times in this book. So read this heavenly letter of joy and be encouraged.

PURPOSE

This could be considered a letter written to friends. Throughout his Philippian letter, Paul speaks of unity and teaches how the church should live as one in the fellowship of Jesus Christ. We also discover in this, the warmest of Paul's letters, many truths about Jesus Christ, his humiliation and exaltation on high. Paul tells us that God seated us in the heavenly realm in his place of authority and power. No wonder we should have joy in our hearts!

AUTHOR AND AUDIENCE

Paul wrote this letter of heavenly joy about AD 60, while Timothy was visiting him in prison. Carried by one of the Philippian church leaders, Epaphroditus, it was delivered to the believers to be read publicly to all. He also wrote it to friends, to partners in the gospel, in the city of Philippi. Paul was motivated to write to these friends because of concerns he had over their disunity, suffering, and opponents. There were also two aspects of his imprisonment that cause him to write the letter: the gospel's advance while he was kept in chains, as well as the gift from the Philippian church. He wrote this letter to express his joyful faith in Christ Jesus while in prison and to communicate his appreciation and love for his generous friends in Philippi.

MAJOR THEMES

The Joyous Gospel of Christ. Paul's main theme in this letter is the gospel, a word that appears more often in this letter than any of his other letters. He is specifically concerned with believers' ongoing relationship with Christ on the other side of their acceptance of the gospel. He is also concerned with the advancement of the gospel, that Jesus' story of rescue and forgiveness goes out into all the world. The words "joy" and "gladness" are found nineteen times in this book!

The Lordship of Christ. At the heart of this letter is the famed *Christ Hymn* (2:6–11)—a soaring melody of worship, adoration, and revelation of the majesty and superiority of Christ as Lord over all. This hymn expresses in lofty, lyrical language the story of Jesus from his preexistent glory to the universal praise of him as Lord paved by his obedience to death on the cross.

The Conduct of Christ. Those who have received and believed the gospel are called to live according to the gospel, to conduct their lives in such a way that they live for Christ. For Paul, such a life is a process of seizing the surpassing worth of Christ and being seized by him. It is also a progressive pursuit of Christ in which we daily die with him in order to experience the fullness of his new life.

The Community of Christ. The community of Christ is the new people of God. Paul contrasts this new people with those in the old community who tried to bring non-Jewish Christians into the circle of Judaism. He also contrasts this community with the world, reminding believers that we are citizens of heaven who submit to the lordship of Christ. Finally, he reminds believers of their unity as brothers and sisters within God's household.

PHILIPPIANS

Heaven's Joy

Introduction

1 From Paul and Timothy,[a] both of us servants of Jesus, the Anointed One. To all his devoted followers in Philippi, including your pastors,[b] and to all the servant-leaders[c] of the church.

²May the blessings of divine grace and supernatural peace that flow from God our wonderful Father, and our Messiah, the Lord Jesus, be upon your lives.

Paul Prays for the Philippians

³⁻⁴My prayers for you are full of praise to God as I give him thanks for you with great joy! *I'm so grateful for our union* ⁵and our enduring partnership that began the first time I presented to you the gospel. ⁶*I pray with great faith for you*, because I'm fully convinced that the One who

---

a 1:1 Timothy was Paul's convert, coworker, and spiritual son. See 1 Tim. 1:2.

b 1:1 Or "guardians," as translated from the Greek. The Aramaic text uses the word *priests*, and could refer to Jewish priests who had received Jesus as the Messiah.

c 1:1 As translated from the Aramaic. The Greek text is "deacons." The word for deacon is actually taken from a Greek compound of the words *dia* and *kovis* that means "to kick up the dust," referring to a servant who is so swift to accomplish his service that he stirs up the dust of the street running to fulfill his duty.

began this gracious work*a* in you will faithfully continue the process of maturing you*b* until the unveiling*c* of our Lord Jesus Christ!

⁷It's no wonder I pray with such confidence, since you have a permanent place in my heart!*d* You have remained partners with me in the wonderful grace *of God* even though I'm here in chains for standing up for the truth of the gospel.*e* ⁸Only God knows how much I dearly love you with the tender affection*f* of Jesus, the Anointed One.

⁹I continue to pray for your love to grow and increase beyond measure, bringing you into the rich revelation of spiritual insight*g* in all things.

---

a 1:6 Or "good [worthwhile] work." Paul uses language here that sounds similar to Gen. 1:2. When God created the heavens and the earth, he declared it to be "good." And now with the new creation life within us, God again sees our growth in grace as something good.

b 1:6 Or "he will see to it that you remain faithful."

c 1:6 Literally "day of Christ." This is the day of his unveiling, his appearing.

d 1:7 Or "since you have given me a permanent place in your hearts."

e 1:7 The Aramaic can be translated "the truth of God's revelation." The Greek can also be translated "for the defense and proof (a possible hendiadys) of the gospel."

f 1:8 Or "mercies."

g 1:9 The Greek word for "insight" (*aisthēsis*) is a hapax legomenon in the New Testament and used numerous times in the Septuagint referring to practical understanding linked to life. It is a word that implies walking out the truth that insight reveals. It could also be translated "experience," or "to experience the reality of something and apply it to life."

[10]This will enable you to choose[a] the most excellent way of all[b]—becoming pure and without offense until the unveiling of Christ.[c] [11]And you will be filled completely with the fruits of righteousness[d] that are found in Jesus, the Anointed One—bringing great praise and glory to God!

Paul's Imprisonment

[12]I want you to know, dear ones,[e] what has happened to me has not hindered, but helped my ministry of preaching the gospel, causing it to expand and spread to many people. [13]For now the elite Roman guards and government officials[f] overseeing my imprisonment have plainly recognized that I am here because of my love for the Anointed One. [14]And what I'm going through has actually caused many believers[g] to become even more courageous in the Lord and to be bold and passionate to preach the Word of God, all because of my chains.

[15]It's true that there are some who preach Christ out of competition and controversy, for they are jealous *over the*

---

a 1:10 The Greek word for "choose" (*dokimazō*) means "to examine, to discern, or approve after testing." It comes from a root word that means "accepted" or "pleasing." So discernment becomes the path to finding what God approves, not simply what God forbids. When love, revelation, and insight overflow into our discernment, we will always be looking for what is excellent and pleasing in God's eyes. We choose what is best, not by law or rules, but by loving discernment.

b 1:10 As translated from the Greek. The Aramaic can be translated "choose those things that bring contentment."

c 1:10 Or "in preparation for the day of Christ." This is the day of his unveiling at his appearing.

d 1:11 Or "the fruit that is righteousness."

e 1:12 Or "my brothers."

f 1:13 Or "Caesar's court."

g 1:14 Or "brothers."

way God has used me. Many others *have purer motives*—they preach with grace and love filling their hearts,[a] [16]because they know I've been destined for the purpose of defending the revelation of God.[b]

[17]Those who preach Christ with ambition and competition are insincere—they just want to add to the hardships of my imprisonment. [18]Yet in spite of all of this I am overjoyed! For what does it matter as long as Christ is being preached? If they preach him with mixed motives or with genuine love, the message of Christ is still being preached. *And I will continue to rejoice* [19]because I know that the lavish supply[c] of the Spirit of Jesus, the Anointed One, and your intercession for me will bring about my deliverance.[d] [20]No matter what, I will continue to hope and passionately cling[e] to Christ, so that he will be openly revealed through me before everyone's eyes.[f] So I will not be ashamed![g] In my life or in my death, Christ will be

---

a 1:15 Or "with goodwill." This translation has borrowed the term "love" from v. 16 and made it explicit here as the purest motive for preaching the gospel.

b 1:16 As translated from the Aramaic. The Greek is "the gospel." The implication from the Aramaic is that some of these preachers (v. 15) had been ordained by Paul.

c 1:19 The Greek word for "supply" can also be translated "festive chorus."

d 1:19 A quotation from Job 13:16 (LXX).

e 1:20 The Greek word is *apokaradokia* and can be translated "with the deepest and intense yearnings," or "the concentrated desire that abandons all other interests with outstretched hands in expectation." It is possible that Paul uses the words "passionately cling," and "hope" as a hendiadys (i.e., "my hope-filled intense expectation"). Romans 8:19 is the only other place in the New Testament where *apokaradokia* is found.

f 1:20 Literally "with uncovered faces." Some interpret it to mean without shame.

g 1:20 See also Rom. 1:16; 2 Cor. 10:8; 1 Peter 4:16; 1 John 2:28.

magnified in me. ²¹My true life is the Anointed One, and dying means gaining more of him.

²²⁻²⁴*So here's my dilemma*: Each day I live means bearing more fruit in my ministry; yet I fervently long to be liberated from this body*ᵃ* and joined fully to Christ. That would suit me fine, but the greatest advantage to you would be that I remain alive. So you can see why I'm torn between the two—I don't know which I prefer.

²⁵Yet deep in my heart I'm confident that I will be spared so I can add to your joy and further strengthen and mature your faith.*ᵇ* ²⁶When I am freed to come to you, my deliverance will give you a reason to boast even more in Jesus Christ.

²⁷Whatever happens, keep living your lives based on the reality of the gospel of Christ. Then when I come to see you, or hear good reports of you, I'll know that you stand united in one Spirit and one passion—celebrating together as conquerors*ᶜ* in the faith of the gospel.*ᵈ* ²⁸And then you will never be shaken or intimidated by the opposition that rises up against us. Your courage will prove to be a sure sign from God of their coming destruction. ²⁹For God has graciously given you the privilege not only to believe in Christ, but also to suffer for him. ³⁰For you have been called by him to endure the conflict in the same way I have endured it—for you know I'm not giving up.

---

a 1:22–24 The Greek uses the word *analyō*, which means "to fold up a tent and depart." Sailors used this word to say, "loose the ship and set sail." And farmers used *analyō* to mean "to unyoke an oxen" (set it free).

b 1:25 Or "that I could help with your pioneer advance and joy in faith." Paul was excited to help them make new pioneer advances in their faith and joy.

c 1:27 As translated literally from the Aramaic. The Greek states "striving side by side with one mind."

d 1:27 Or "his revelation."

Joined Together in Perfect Unity

2 Look at how much encouragement[a] you've found in your relationship with the Anointed One! You are filled to overflowing with his comforting love. You have experienced a deepening friendship with the Holy Spirit and have felt his tender affection and mercy.[b]

²So I'm asking you, my friends, that you be joined together in perfect unity—with one heart, one passion, and united in one love. Walk together[c] with one harmonious purpose and you will fill my heart with unbounded joy.

³Be free from pride-filled opinions, *for they will only harm your cherished unity*. Don't allow self-promotion to hide in your hearts, but in authentic humility put others first and view others as more important than yourselves. ⁴Abandon every display of selfishness. Possess a greater concern for what matters to others instead of your own interests. ⁵And consider the example that Jesus, the Anointed One, has set before us. Let his mindset become your motivation.

The Example of Jesus Christ

⁶He existed in the form of God, yet he gave no thought to seizing equality with God as his supreme prize.[d] ⁷Instead he emptied himself of his outward glory by reducing himself to the form of a lowly servant. He became human! ⁸He humbled himself and became vulnerable, choosing to be revealed as a man and was obedient.[e] *He was a*

---

a 2:1 The Greek word *paraklesis* can also mean "exhortation" or "comfort."

b 2:1 Or "sympathies." The Aramaic can be translated "your heart flutters with his compassion."

c 2:2 Or "Be like-minded."

d 2:6 Or "as something to be exploited."

e 2:8 See also John 5:19.

perfect example, even in his death—a criminal's death by crucifixion![a]

[9]Because of that obedience, God exalted him and multiplied his greatness! He has now been given the greatest of all names!

[10]The authority of the name of Jesus causes every knee to bow in reverence! Everything and everyone will one day submit to this name—in the heavenly realm, in the earthly realm, and in the demonic realm.[b] [11]And every tongue will proclaim in every language: "Jesus Christ is Lord Yahweh,"[c] bringing glory and honor to God, his Father![d]

---

a 2:8 Notice the seven steps Christ took from the throne to the cross in vv. 7–8: (1) He emptied himself. (2) He became a servant. (3) He became human. (4) He humbled himself. (5) He became vulnerable and was revealed as a man. (6) He was obedient until his death. (7) He died a criminal's death on the cross.

b 2:10 Or "heaven, earth, and under the earth."

c 2:11 As translated from the Aramaic. The Greek text uses the word *kurios*, which is not the highest name for God. *Yahweh* (Hebrew) or *Jehovah* (Latin) is the highest name. *Kurios* is a title also used for false gods, land owners, merchants, and nobles. The Greek language has no equal to the sacred name (the tetragrammaton—*YHWH*), Yahweh. Only Hebrew and Aramaic have that equivalent. This verse makes it clear that the name given to Jesus at his exaltation was "Lord Jehovah" or "Lord Yahweh." The Hebrew name for Jesus is *Yeshua* (lit. "God is a Saving-Cry"), which bears and reveals the name Yahweh. Jesus carries the name and reputation of his Father, Yahweh, within him. See John 17:11.

d 2:11 Note the seven steps of exaltation that God gave Jesus after the cross: (1) God exalted him and multiplied his greatness. (2) He possesses the greatest name of all. (3) His sovereign authority will cause every knee to bow. (4) God decreed that everyone in heaven will bow in worship of the God-Man. (5) God decreed that every demonic being will bow to the God-Man. (6) God decreed that every tongue will proclaim that Jesus Christ is Lord Yahweh! (7) God received the glory and honor of sharing his throne with the God-Man.

Believers Shine Like Lights in the World

[12]My beloved ones, just like you've always listened to everything I've taught you in the past, I'm asking you now to keep following my instructions as though I were right there with you. Now you must continue to make this new life fully manifested as you live[a] in the holy awe of God—which brings you trembling into his presence. [13]God will continually revitalize you, implanting within you the passion to do what pleases him.[b]

[14]Live a cheerful life, without complaining or division among yourselves. [15]For then you will be seen as innocent,[c] faultless, and pure children of God, even though you live in the midst of a brutal and perverse culture.[d] For you will appear among them as shining lights[e] in the universe, [16]holding out[f] the words of *eternal* life.[g]

I haven't labored among you for nothing, for *your lives are the fruit of my ministry* and will be my glorious boast at the unveiling[h] of Christ!

[17]But I will rejoice even if my life is poured out like a liquid offering to God over your sacrificial and surrendered

---

a 2:12 The Aramaic can be translated "push through the service of your life" or "work the work of your life."

b 2:13 The Aramaic can be translated "to accomplish the good things you desire to do."

c 2:15 Or "mature."

d 2:15 See Deut. 32:5–6.

e 2:15 The Aramaic can be translated "the enlightened ones."

f 2:16 Or "holding fast to the words of eternal life."

g 2:16 The Aramaic can be translated "you stand in the place of life to them." The Greek text means "holding out to them the word of life."

h 2:16 Or "day."

lives of faith.*^a ¹⁸And so no matter what happens to me, you should rejoice in ecstatic celebration with me!

The Example of Timothy

¹⁹Yet I'm trusting in our Lord Jesus that I may send Timothy to you soon, so I can be refreshed when I find out how you're doing. ²⁰Timothy is like no other. He carries the same passion for your welfare that I carry in my heart. ²¹For it seems as though everyone else is busy seeking what is best for themselves instead of the things that are most important to our Lord Jesus Christ. ²²You already know about his excellent reputation, since he has served alongside me as a loyal son in the work of ministry. ²³After I see what transpires with me he's the one I will send to you to bless you. ²⁴And I'm trusting in my Lord to return to you in due time.

²⁵But for now, I feel a stirring in my heart to send Epaphroditus*^b back to you immediately. He's a friend to me and a wonderful brother and fellow soldier who has worked with me *as we serve as ministers of the gospel.* And you sent him as your apostle to minister to me in my need. ²⁶But now he is grieved to know that you found out he had been sick, so he longs to return and comfort you in this.

²⁷It's true he almost died, but God showed him mercy and healed him. And I'm so thankful to God for his healing, as I was spared from having the sorrow of losing him on top of all my other troubles! ²⁸So you can see why I'm

---

a 2:17 The interpretation of this verse is difficult; it is speaking about Paul's willingness to be a love offering for the Philippians if that's what God desired. There is a powerful figure of speech contained in the Aramaic, literally translated as "though I imbibe the wine poured over the offering." This is a metaphor of Paul shedding his blood one day because of his love for the Philippians. Indeed, Paul was later martyred for his faith.

b 2:25 His name means "charming."

delighted to send him to you now. I know that you're anxious to see him and rejoice in his healing, and it encourages me to know how happy you'll be to have him back.

²⁹So warmly welcome him home in the Lord,ᵃ with joyous love, and esteem him highly, for people like him deserve it. ³⁰Because of me, he put his life on the line, despising the danger, so that he could provide for me with what you couldn't, since you were so far away. And he did it all because of his ministry for Christ.

A Call to Rejoice and a Warning

3 My beloved ones, don't ever limit your joy or fail to rejoice in the wonderful experience of knowing our Lord Jesus!

I don't mind repeating what I've already written you because it protects you—²beware of those religious hypocritesᵇ who teach that you should be circumcised to please God. ³For we have already experienced "heart-circumcision," and we worship God in the power and freedom of the Holy Spirit, *not in laws and religious duties*. We are those who boast in what Jesus Christ has done, and not in what we can accomplish in our own strength.

⁴It's true that *I once relied on all that I had become*. I had a reason to boast and impress people with my accomplishments—more than others—for my pedigree was impeccable.

---

a 2:29 Or "Lord Yahweh."

b 3:2 Literally "dogs," which is a figure of speech for religious hypocrites.

The Example of Paul

[5]I was born a true Hebrew of the heritage of Israel[a] as the son of a Jewish man from the tribe of Benjamin.[b] I was circumcised eight days after my birth and *was raised in the strict tradition of Orthodox Judaism*, living a separated[c] and devout life as a Pharisee. [6]And concerning the righteousness of the Torah,[d] no one surpassed me; I was without a peer. Furthermore, as a fiery defender of the truth, I persecuted the messianic believers with religious zeal.

[7]Yet all of the accomplishments that I once took credit for, I've now forsaken them and I regard it all as nothing compared to the delight of experiencing Jesus Christ as my Lord! [8]To truly know him meant letting go of everything from my past and throwing all my boasting on the garbage heap. It's all like a pile of manure to me now, so that I may be enriched in the reality of knowing Jesus Christ and embrace him as Lord in all of his greatness.

[9]My passion is to be consumed with him and not cling to my own "righteousness" based in keeping the written Law. My only "righteousness" will be his, based on the faithfulness of Jesus Christ—the very righteousness that comes from God. [10]And I continually long to know the wonders of Jesus and to experience the overflowing power of his resurrection working in me. I will be one with him in his sufferings and become like him in his death. [11]Only then will I be able to experience complete oneness with him in his resurrection from the realm of death.

---

a 3:5 This meant that he could trace his family line all the way back to Abraham. There is also an inference that Paul spoke Hebrew-Aramaic as his native tongue and did not adopt Greek customs.

b 3:5 The tribe of Benjamin was honored as the tribe most loyal to the house of David. *Benjamin* means "son of my right hand."

c 3:5 A Pharisee was known as a "separated one," who religiously followed all the laws of Judaism.

d 3:6 Or "the written law."

[12]I admit that I haven't yet acquired the absolute fullness that I'm pursuing, but I run with passion *into his abundance* so that I may reach the purpose for which Christ Jesus laid hold of me to make me his own. [13]I don't depend on my own strength to accomplish this;[a] however I do have one compelling focus: I forget all of the past as I fasten my heart to the future instead. [14]I run straight for the divine invitation of reaching the heavenly goal and gaining the victory-prize through the anointing of Jesus. [15]So let all who are fully mature have this same passion, and if anyone is not yet gripped by these desires,[b] God will reveal it to them. [16]And let us all advance together to reach this victory-prize, following one path with one passion.

[17]My beloved friends, imitate my walk with God and follow all those who walk according to the way of life we modeled before you. [18]For there are many who live by different standards. As I've warned you many times (I weep as I write these words), they are enemies of the cross of the Anointed One and [19]doom awaits them. Their god has possessed them and made them mute.[c] Their boast is in their shameful lifestyles and their minds are in the dirt.[d]

[20]But we are a colony[e] of heaven on earth as we cling tightly to our life-giver, the Lord Jesus Christ, [21]who will transform our humble bodies[f] and transfigure us into the

---

a 3:13 This phrase is translated from the Aramaic. The Greek text states "I, myself, have not taken possession of it."

b 3:15 The Aramaic can be translated "those who don't run this way, God will reveal it to them."

c 3:19 Translated from the Aramaic. The Greek states "their god is their belly," which is meaningless to the average English speaker.

d 3:19 Translated from the Aramaic. It literally means "their conscience is in the ground."

e 3:20 Or "citizenship," or "commonwealth."

f 3:21 Or "the body of our humility."

identical likeness of his glorified body.[a] And using his matchless power, he continually subdues everything to himself.[b]

Living in Harmony with One Another

4 My dear and precious friends, whom I deeply love, you have truly become my glorious joy and crown of reward. Now arise[c] in the fullness of your union with our Lord.

[2]And I plead with Euodia and Syntyche to settle their disagreement and be restored with one mind in our Lord.[d] [3]I would like my dear friend and burden-bearer[e] to help resolve this issue, for both women have diligently labored with me for the prize and helped in spreading the revelation of the gospel,[f] along with Clement[g] and the rest of my coworkers. All of their names are written in the Book of Life.

---

a 3:21 Or "the body of his glory."

b 3:21 The Aramaic can be translated "everyone is in submission to him."

c 4:1 The Aramaic word *arise* implies "resurrection." The Greek is "stand fast."

d 4:2 In every church there is often found conflict in relationships. Paul seeks to encourage these two dear women to resolve all their disagreements. Their names give us a clue. Euodia comes from a word that means "a fair journey." Syntyche comes from a word that can mean "an accident." Along our fair journey we may collide with another, but God always has grace for restoration.

e 4:3 Or "Syzygos," possibly a name, however there is no record of anyone in classical or biblical Greek with this name. Some believe that Syzygos was one of the pastors of the church at Philippi.

f 4:3 The Aramaic can also be translated "God's kingdom realm."

g 4:3 Clement was one of the men who led the church in Philippi. His name means "mild" or "merciful."

⁴Be cheerful with joyous celebration in every season of life. Let your joy overflow! ⁵And let gentleness*ᵃ* be seen in every relationship, for our Lord is ever near.*ᵇ*

⁶Don't be pulled in different directions or worried about a thing. Be saturated in prayer throughout each day, offering your faith-filled requests before God with overflowing gratitude. Tell him every detail of your life, ⁷then God's wonderful peace that transcends human understanding, will guard your heart and mind through Jesus Christ. ⁸Keep your thoughts continually fixed on all that is authentic and real, honorable and admirable, beautiful and respectful, pure and holy, merciful and kind. And fasten your thoughts on every glorious work of God,*ᶜ* praising him always. ⁹*Put into practice the example* of all that you have heard from me or seen in my life and the God of peace will be with you in all things.

Paul Thanks the Philippians for Their Support

¹⁰My heart overflows with joy when I think of how you demonstrated love to me *by your financial support of my ministry*. For even though you have so little, you still continue to help me at every opportunity. ¹¹I'm not telling you this because I'm in need, for I have learned to be satisfied in any circumstance.*ᵈ* ¹²⁻¹³I know what it means to lack,*ᵉ* and I know what it means to experience overwhelming abundance. For I'm trained in the secret of overcoming all things, whether in fullness or in hunger. And I find that the strength of Christ's explosive power infuses me to conquer every difficulty.*ᶠ*

---

a 4:5 The Greek word means "fairness;" the Aramaic "humility."
b 4:5 Or "approaching."
c 4:8 The Aramaic can be translated "acts of glorification."
d 4:11 Or "to give up everything I have."
e 4:12–13 Or "be humbled."
f 4:12–13 Or "to master all things."

[14]You've so graciously provided for my essential needs during this season of difficulty. [15]For I want you to know that the Philippian church was the only church that supported me in the beginning as I went out to preach the gospel. You were the only church that sowed into me financially,[a] [16]and when I was in Thessalonica, you supported me for well over a year.[b]

[17]I mention this not because I'm requesting a gift, but so that the fruit of your generosity may bring you an abundant reward. [18]I now have all I need—more than enough—I'm abundantly satisfied! For I've received the gift you sent by Epaphroditus and viewed it as a sweet sacrifice, perfumed with the fragrance *of your faithfulness*, which is so pleasing to God!

[19]I am convinced that my God will fully satisfy every need you have, *for I have seen* the abundant riches of glory *revealed to me* through Jesus Christ! [20]And God our Father will receive all the glory and the honor throughout the eternity of eternities! Amen!

[21]Give my warm greetings to all the believers in Christ Jesus. [22]All the brothers and sisters that are here with me send their loving greetings, especially the converts from Caesar's household.

[23]May the grace and favor of our Lord Jesus Christ be with your spirit!

---

a 4:15 The Aramaic can be translated "accounts of planting and giving."

b 4:16 As translated from the Aramaic. The Greek means "twice you sent gifts."

COLOSSIANS

Introduction

AT A GLANCE

Author: The apostle Paul
Audience: The church of Colossae
Date: AD 60–61
Type of Literature: A letter
Major Themes: Christ, the church, the gospel, and the Christian life
Outline:

Letter Opening — 1:1–2:5
Letter Theme: Christ-Centered Living — 2:6–7
Threats to Christ-Centered Living — 2:8–23
Living a Christ-Centered Life — 3:1–4:6
Letter Closing — 4:7–18

ABOUT COLOSSIANS

What a glorious hope lives within us! This is the theme of Paul's masterpiece written to the church of Colossae—our hope of glory!

The beauty and revelation that comes into us when we receive the truth of this letter is astounding. The Holy Spirit hands to us many wonderful nuggets of gold here. The heavenly hope of glory, the mystery hidden and reserved for this generation, is Jesus our anointed Messiah.

Paul penned this letter while in a prison cell. When hope was absent in his environment, Paul rediscovered it in his enjoyment of Christ within himself. No matter where you live or what surrounds you in this moment, there is a burning hope inside your soul that does more than just carry you through—it releases the heavenly Christ within. Great comfort and encouragement can be found by reading the letter to the Colossians.

Written about AD 60, Paul seeks to focus on the wonderful hope of the gospel and reminds the believers to not turn aside or fall victim to those who would minimize Christ and lead the church into empty philosophies and humanism. Already, there were many false teachers and cults that were forming and deceiving new believers and drawing them away from the supremacy of Christ. Many have noted that of all Paul's letters, Colossians speaks more of the importance of Christ than any other.

Nearly everyone who has studied Colossians would agree that the summary of this letter can be found in 1:18–19: "He is the Head of his body, which is the church. And since he is the beginning and the firstborn heir in resurrection, he is the most exalted One, holding first place in everything. For God is satisfied to have all his fullness dwelling in Christ."

We can never be moved away from our glorious Head, Jesus Christ! To see him is to see the fullness of the Father and the fullness of the Holy Spirit. How we love this firstborn heir of all things!

PURPOSE

The major reason why Paul wrote this letter was to equip the Colossian church to fend off false teaching and help them resist false teachers within the community. It seems as though certain Christians in the city had believed and were promoting a version of Christianity that threatened orthodox beliefs and practices that stood in contrast to what the Colossian church had received from Epaphras. Paul judged this version to not only be deficient but dangerous. He penned this letter to remind believers of the wonderful hope of the gospel and not to turn aside or fall victim to those who would minimize Christ and lead the church into empty philosophies and humanism.

AUTHOR AND AUDIENCE

Although the apostle Paul wrote this letter to the church of Colossae, we do not believe he was the one who started this church, nor had he ever been to the city. It was most likely the result of Paul's three-year ministry in Ephesus, which was less than a hundred miles away. So effective was Paul's preaching and teaching that his converts spread the message out of Ephesus throughout the region known as Asia Minor. Most likely it was Epaphras who was the church planter in the Lycus Valley, which included the cities of Laodicea, Hieropolis, and Colossae.

Although Paul had never visited their city, he had heard of the believers of Colossae and began to pray for them that they would advance and become the fullness of Christ on the earth. Perhaps the new converts had met first in the home of Philemon until they outgrew the "house church." How tenderly Paul speaks to them, as a father in the faith, to motivate them to keep their hearts and beliefs free from error. The church today needs to hear these truths.

MAJOR THEMES

The Supremacy and Centrality of Christ. The key theme to Paul's letter to the church at Colossae is the supremacy and centrality of Christ. One of the clearest pictures we have of this theme is the famed "Christ Hymn" of 1:15–20. Colossians makes it clear that in reigning supreme Jesus is himself God. As God he reigns over all creation. Paul also makes it clear that Jesus is all sufficient for our spiritual life, and should reign supreme at its center.

The Body of Christ. One of the most unique aspects of this letter is Paul's description of the church as Christ's "body." He presents Christ as the church's ruler, who has authority over her and who also sustains her. And as Christ's body, we are the continuing presence of Christ on the earth; through the church the mission of Christ is revealed and advanced.

The True Gospel. The major purpose for Paul's letter was to confront false teachers and their false gospel. Apparently, they were adding to the gospel Epaphras taught—mixing Jewish legalism, human tradition, and angel worship. Paul urges the Colossians to reject this religious enslavement and remember the true message of Christ and his lasting hope: "Never be shaken from the hope of the gospel you have believed in" (Col. 1:23).

The Christian Life. Using the metaphor of a body, Paul teaches that our life as Christians must be rooted in Christ—he is the Head, after all. He is the one who empowers us and renews us; we have our entire existence in him! Since it is through Christ we live as Christians, a "rules-oriented" lifestyle dictated by humans will not lead to spiritual growth.

COLOSSIANS

Heaven's Hope

Introduction

1 *Dear friends* in Colossae,

[1-2]*My name is* Paul and I have been chosen by Jesus Christ to be his apostle, by the calling and destined purpose of God. My colleague, Timothy, and I send this letter to all the holy believers who have been united to Jesus as beloved followers of the Messiah. May God, our true Father, release upon your lives the riches of his kind favor and heavenly peace through the Lord Jesus, the Anointed One.

Paul Prays for the Colossians

[3]Every time we pray for you our hearts overflow with thanksgiving to Father God, the Father of our Lord Jesus Christ. [4]For we have heard of your devoted lives of faith in Christ Jesus and your tender love toward all his holy believers. [5]Your faith and love rise within you as you access all the treasures of your inheritance[a] stored up in the heavenly realm. For the revelation of the true gospel is as real today as the day you first heard of our glorious hope, now that you have believed in the truth of the gospel.

[6]*This is the wonderful message that* is being spread everywhere, powerfully changing hearts throughout the earth, just like it has changed you! Every believer of this good

---

a 1:5 Or "hope."

news bears the fruit of eternal life as they experience the reality of God's grace.

[7]Our beloved coworker, Epaphras,[a] was there from the beginning to thoroughly teach you the astonishing revelation of the gospel, and he serves you faithfully as Christ's representative. [8]He's informed us of the many wonderful ways love is being demonstrated through your lives by the empowerment of the Holy Spirit.

[9]Since we first heard about you, we've kept you always in our prayers that you would receive the perfect knowledge of God's pleasure[b] over your lives, making you reservoirs of every kind of wisdom and spiritual understanding. [10]We pray that you would walk in the ways of true righteousness, pleasing God in every good thing you do. Then you'll become fruit-bearing branches, yielding to his life, and maturing in the rich experience of knowing God in his fullness! [11]And we pray that you would be energized with all his explosive power from the realm of his magnificent glory, filling you with great hope.[c]

[12]*Your hearts can soar with* joyful gratitude when you think of how God made you worthy to receive the glorious inheritance freely given to us by living in the light.[d] [13]He has rescued us completely from the tyrannical rule[e] of darkness and has translated us into the kingdom realm of his beloved Son. [14]For in the Son all our sins are

---

a 1:7 The church of Colossae was not planted by Paul but by Epaphras. His name means "lovely." He imparted to the church faith and love, praying always for them. See Col. 4:12.

b 1:9 Or "experience God's will for your lives." The Greek word *thelema*, can also mean "desire" or "pleasure."

c 1:11 As translated from the Aramaic. The Greek text means "patient endurance."

d 1:12 Or "by enlightening us."

e 1:13 Or "authority."

canceled and we have the release of redemption *through his very blood.*

The Supremacy of Christ

[15]He is the divine portrait, the true likeness of the invisible God, and the firstborn heir of all creation. [16]For in him was created the universe of things, both in the heavenly realm and on the earth, all that is seen and all that is unseen. Every seat of power, realm of government, principality, and authority—it all exists through him and for his purpose! [17]He existed before anything was made, and now everything finds completion in him.

[18]He is the Head of his body, which is the church. And since he is the beginning and the firstborn heir in resurrection,[a] he is the most exalted One, holding first place[b] in everything. [19]For God is satisfied to have all his fullness[c] dwelling in Christ. [20]And by the blood of his cross, everything in heaven and earth is brought back to himself—*back to its original intent, restored to innocence again!*[d]

Made Holy through Christ

[21-22]Even though you were once distant from him, living in the shadows of your evil thoughts and actions, he reconnected you back to himself. *He released his supernatural peace to you* through the sacrifice of his own body as the sin-payment on your behalf so that you would dwell in his presence. And now there is nothing between you and

---

a 1:18 Literally "from the dead."

b 1:18 In the Greek text this is a title, "the Holder of First Place" or "the Superior One."

c 1:19 This includes all the fullness of God, the fullness of his plan for our lives, and the full image of God being restored into our hearts.

d 1:20 It literally means "back to himself." Some scholars believe that Col. 1:15–20 is actually lyrics of an ancient hymn sung in the churches.

Father God, for he sees you as holy, flawless, and restored,[a] [23]if indeed you continue to advance in faith, assured of a firm foundation to grow upon. Never be shaken from the hope of the gospel you have believed in. And this is the glorious news I preach all over the world.

The Divine Mystery

[24]I can even celebrate the sorrows I have experienced on your behalf; for as I join with you in your difficulties, it helps you to discover what lacks *in your understanding*[b] of the sufferings Jesus Christ experienced for his body, the church. [25]This is the very reason I've been made a minister by the authority of God and a servant to his body, so that in his detailed plan I would fully equip you with the Word of God.

[26]There is a divine mystery—a secret surprise that has been concealed from the world for generations, but now it's being revealed, unfolded and manifested for every holy believer to experience. [27]Living within you is the Christ who floods you with the expectation of glory! This mystery of Christ, embedded within us, becomes a heavenly treasure chest of hope filled with the riches of glory for his people, and God wants everyone to know it!

[28-29]Christ is our message! We preach to awaken hearts and bring every person into the full understanding of truth. It has become my inspiration and passion in ministry to labor with a tireless intensity, with his power flowing through me, to present to every believer the revelation of being his perfect one in Jesus Christ.

---

a 1:21–22 Or "without an indictment."

b 1:24 The text contains an ellipsis that is completed by this translation. The sufferings of Christ were complete, sufficient to transfer righteousness and forgiveness to every believer. Paul's sufferings were meant to be an example of Christ and a testimony to his converts that his ministry was sincere.

Paul's Love for the Colossians

2 I wish you could know how much I have struggled[a] for you and for the church in Laodicea, and for the many other friends I've yet to meet. [2]I am contending for you that your hearts will be wrapped in the comfort of heaven and woven together into love's fabric. This will give you access[b] to all the riches of God as you experience the revelation of God's great mystery—Christ.

[3]For our spiritual wealth is in him, like hidden treasure waiting to be discovered—heaven's wisdom and endless riches of revelation knowledge.

[4]I want you to know this so that no one will come and lead you into error[c] through their persuasive arguments and clever words. [5]Even though I'm separated from you geographically, my spirit is present there with you. And I'm overjoyed to see how disciplined[d] and deeply committed you are because you have such a solid faith in Christ, the Anointed One.

New Life in Christ

[6]In the same way you received Jesus our Lord and Messiah by faith, continue your journey of faith, progressing further into your union with him! [7]Your spiritual roots go deeply into his life as you are continually infused with strength, encouraged in every way. For you are

---

a 2:1 The Greek word *agon* (from which we get "agony") means an intense conflict and struggle. This could imply Paul's apostolic intercession for them.

b 2:2 Or in the Aramaic "approach."

c 2:4 By implication, this "error" would be the teaching that Jesus is not enough, adding something to the all-sufficient Christ.

d 2:5 The Greek text literally means "unbroken battle formation." The Aramaic can be translated "organized" or "principled."

established in the faith you have absorbed and enriched by your devotion to him!*a*

⁸Beware that no one distracts you or intimidates you*b* *in their attempt to lead you away from Christ's fullness* by pretending to be full of wisdom when they're filled with endless arguments of human logic. For they operate with humanistic and clouded judgments based on the mindset of this world system, and not the anointed truths of the Anointed One.

⁹For he is the complete fullness of deity living in human form. ¹⁰And our own completeness is now found in him. We are completely filled *with God* as Christ's fullness overflows within us. He is the Head*c* of every kingdom and authority in the universe!

¹¹Through our union with him we have experienced circumcision of heart. All of the guilt and power of sin*d* has been cut away and is now extinct because of what Christ, the Anointed One, has accomplished for us.

¹²For we've been buried with him into his death. Our "baptism into death" also means we were raised with him when we believed in God's resurrection power, the power that raised him from death's realm. ¹³This "realm of death" describes our former state, for we were held in sin's grasp.*e* But now, we've been resurrected out of that "realm of death" never to return, for we are forever alive and forgiven of all our sins!

---

a 2:7 As translated from the Aramaic. The Greek states "overflowing with gratitude."

b 2:8 The Aramaic can be translated "strips you naked." The Greek states "takes you captive."

c 2:10 Or "Source."

d 2:11 The Aramaic can be translated "flesh of sin." The Greek means "body of the natural realm."

e 2:13 Literally "the uncircumcision of your flesh."

¹⁴He canceled out every legal violation we had on our record and the old arrest warrant that stood to indict us. He erased it all—our sins, our stained*ᵃ* soul—he deleted it all *and they cannot be retrieved*! Everything we once were in Adam*ᵇ* has been placed onto his cross and nailed permanently there as a public display of cancellation.

¹⁵Then Jesus made a public spectacle of all the powers and principalities of darkness, stripping away from them every weapon and all their spiritual authority and power*ᶜ* to accuse us. And by the power of the cross, Jesus led them around as prisoners in a procession of triumph. *He was not their prisoner; they were his!ᵈ*

---

a 2:14 This "stained soul" has been erased of its filth. The word "erased" explicitly holds the concept of removal of stains. This would mean the nature of Adam has been erased and the nature of Christ has been embedded into us. We are totally set free from every trace of sin by the power of the blood of Jesus Christ.

b 2:14 The Aramaic can be translated "from our midst." This would refer to all that was within us—the core of our past life and its memories of failure and disobedience. A new DNA has been embedded now within us through the cross and resurrection life of Christ.

c 2:15 Literally "governments and authorities."

d 2:15 Implied by the obvious irony in the Greek. The Aramaic text has a phrase that is not found in Greek manuscripts. The Aramaic can be translated "having *put off his body*, he stripped principalities and powers and shamed them openly." This implies that between the day of crucifixion and the day of resurrection while in the spirit-realm, Jesus destroyed death, the powers of darkness, and every work of the enemy through the blood of his cross. All the enemy's weapons have been stripped away from him and now the church has authority in Christ to enforce this triumph upon the dethroned rulers of this world. However, an alternate translation of the Aramaic could be "after *sending out his body* [apostles, prophets, evangelists, pastors, teachers, believers], they enforced his triumph to all the thrones and authorities, putting them all to public shame by the manifestation of himself [in them]."

Liberty in Christ

[16]So why would you allow anyone[a] to judge you because of what you eat or drink, or insist that you keep the feasts, observe new moon celebrations, or the Sabbath? [17]All of these were but a prophetic shadow and the evidence of what would be fulfilled,[b] for the body[c] is now Christ!

[18]Don't let anyone disqualify you from your prize! Don't let their pretended sincerity fool you as they deliberately lead you into their initiation of angel worship.[d] For they take pleasure in pretending to be experts of something they know nothing about. Their reasoning is meaningless and comes only from their own opinions. [19]They refuse to take hold of the true source.

---

a 2:16 The Aramaic text implies "any unbeliever."

b 2:17 The revelation of the Old Testament is so rich when we understand that its shadow is displaced by the body of Christ, the full revelation of who he is. The shadow only reflects the substance of what has now been fulfilled.

c 2:17 Or "substance."

d 2:18 In the first century AD, there was a mystical Jewish religion called Merkabah Mysticism, or Chariot Mysticism, in which the initiate would seek to go into the palace of God through meditation and enter into his chariot-throne. His was the innermost palace of seven concentric heavenly palaces surrounding his chariot-throne. At each "palace" or level there would be a fierce protecting angel, acting as a mediator who had to be placated by angel worship, which would enable the worshiper to enter the next level. There were also ancient polytheistic folk religions that worshiped and invoked angels. These were entirely forbidden paths for believers in Jesus, and Paul warned them of that in this letter.

But we receive directly from him, and his life supplies[a] vitality into every part of his body through the joining ligaments connecting us all as one. *He is the divine Head who guides his body* and causes it to grow by the supernatural power of God.[b]

[20]For you were included in the death of Christ and have died with him to the religious system and powers of this world. Don't retreat back to being bullied by the standards and opinions of religion—[21]*for example, their strict requirements*, "You can't associate with that person!" or, "Don't eat that!" or, "You can't touch that!" [22]These are the doctrines of men and corrupt customs that are worthless to help you spiritually. [23]For though they may appear to possess the promise of wisdom in their submission to God through the deprivation of their physical bodies, it is actually nothing more than empty rules rooted in religious rituals!

One with Christ in Glory

3 Christ's resurrection is your resurrection too. This is why we are to yearn for all that is above, for that's where Christ sits enthroned at the place of all power, honor, and authority![c] [2]Yes, *feast on all the treasures of the*

---

a 2:19 The Greek word used here is *epichoregeo*, which interestingly can be translated as "to lead the chorus," or "choir director." It was used to denote a person who paid for the expenses of a Greek drama, and who supplied all their needs throughout its production. Similarly, Jesus tunes us up to heaven's notes, and draws out of us the melody of his divine symphony. He supplies the music to us, and imparts the wisdom for us to play it under his direction. This is the artful picture of how Jesus orchestrates his body with its many members.

b 2:19 Or "makes it grow with the discipline from God."

c 3:1 The "right hand of God," is an obvious metaphor for the place of power, authority, honor, and glory.

heavenly realm and fill your thoughts with heavenly realities, and not with the distractions of the natural realm.

[3]Your crucifixion[a] with Christ has severed the tie to this life, and now your true life is hidden away in God in Christ. [4]And as Christ himself is seen for who he really is, who you really are will also be revealed, for you are now one with him in his glory!

New Creation Life

[5]Live as one who has died to every form of sexual sin and impurity. Live as one who has died to the desires for forbidden things,[b] including the desire for wealth, which is the essence of idol worship. [6]When you live in these vices you ignite the anger of God against these acts of disobedience.[c]

[7-8]That's how you once behaved, characterized by your evil deeds. But now it's time to eliminate them from your lives once and for all—anger, fits of rage, all forms of hatred,[d] cursing,[e] filthy speech, [9]and lying.[f] Lay aside[g] your old Adam-self with its masquerade and disguise.

[10]For you have acquired new creation life which is continually being renewed into the likeness of the One who created you; giving you the full revelation of God. [11]In this

---

a 3:3 The Aramaic could be translated "Your death and your life are both hidden with the Messiah in God."

b 3:5 The Aramaic word implies "magic."

c 3:6 As translated from the Aramaic. The Greek states "the sons of disobedience," but it is actually the "deeds" which are punished as seen in verses 7–9. The Aramaic word used here is a homonym that can mean either "sons" or "deeds," which may explain the variation within Greek manuscripts.

d 3:7–8 Including self-hatred.

e 3:7–8 As translated from the Aramaic. The Greek means "slander."

f 3:9 Or "living a lie."

g 3:9 As translated from the Greek. The Aramaic has a command, "take off the old life."

new creation life, your nationality makes no difference, nor your ethnicity, education, nor economic status—*they matter nothing.* For it is Christ that means everything as he lives in every one of us![a]

Love One Another

[12]You are always and dearly loved by God! So robe yourself *with virtues of God*, since you have been divinely chosen to be holy. Be merciful as you endeavor to understand others, and be compassionate, showing kindness toward all. Be gentle and humble, unoffendable in your patience with others. [13]Tolerate the weaknesses of those in the family of faith, forgiving one another in the same way you have been graciously forgiven by Jesus Christ. If you find fault with someone, release this same gift of forgiveness to them. [14]For love is supreme and must flow through each of these virtues. Love becomes the mark[b] of true maturity.[c]

[15]Let your heart be always guided[d] by the peace of the Anointed One, who called you to peace as part of his one body. And always be thankful.

[16]Let the word of Christ live[e] in you richly, flooding you with all wisdom. *Apply the Scriptures* as you teach and instruct one another with the Psalms, and with festive praises,[f] and with prophetic songs given to you spontaneously by the Spirit, so sing to God with all your hearts!

---

a 3:11 Or "there is neither Jew or Scythians, circumcision or uncircumcision, neither Greek nor barbarian, neither slave nor free, but the Messiah is all and in all."

b 3:14 The Aramaic can be translated "the girdle of maturity."

c 3:14 Or "perfection."

d 3:15 The Greek literally means "let peace be the umpire of your minds."

e 3:16 Or "grow."

f 3:16 Or "hymns."

[17]Let every activity[a] of your lives and every word[b] that comes from your lips be drenched with the beauty of our Lord Jesus, the Anointed One. And bring your constant praise to God the Father *because of what Christ has done for you!*

Loving Relationships

[18]Let every wife be supportive and tenderly devoted[c] to her husband, *for this is a beautiful illustration* of our devotion to Christ. [19]Let every husband be filled with cherishing love for his wife and never be insensitive[d] toward her.

[20]Let the children respect and pay attention to their parents in everything for this pleases our Lord Jesus. [21]And fathers, don't have unrealistic expectations[e] for your children or else they may become discouraged.

[22]Let every employee listen well and follow the instructions of their employer, not just when their employers are watching, and not in pretense, but faithful in all things. For we are to live our lives with pure hearts in the constant awe and wonder of our Lord God.

[23]Put your heart and soul into every activity you do, as though you are doing it for the Lord himself and not merely for others.

[24]For we know that we will receive a reward, an inheritance from the Lord, as we serve the Lord Yahweh,[f] the Anointed One! [25]A disciple will be repaid for what he has

---

a 3:17 The Aramaic can be translated "commitment."

b 3:17 The Aramaic can be translated "oath."

c 3:18 The Greek word, *hupotasso*, can be translated "submitted," "attached," or "supportive."

d 3:19 Or "bitter."

e 3:21 Or "exasperate your children."

f 3:24 Although absent in the Greek manuscripts, the Aramaic text makes it abundantly clear that it is Jesus Christ who is the Lord God (Yahweh). See also Luke 2:11.

learned and followed,*a* for God pays no attention to the titles or prestige of men.

4 Employers, treat your workers with equality and justice as you know that you also have a Lord and Master in heaven *who is watching you.*

A Life of Prayer

²Be faithful to pray as intercessors who are fully alert and giving thanks *to God.* ³And please pray for me, that God will open a door of opportunity for us to preach the revelation of the mystery of Christ, for whose sake I am imprisoned. ⁴Pray that I would unfold and reveal fully this mystery, for that is my delightful assignment.*b*

⁵Walk in the wisdom of God as you live before the unbelievers,*c* and make it your duty*d* to make him known. ⁶Let every word you speak be drenched with grace*e* and tempered with truth and clarity.*f* For then you will be prepared to give a respectful answer to anyone who asks about your faith.

Paul's Coworkers

⁷⁻⁸Tychicus will tell you about what is happening with me. I have sent him to you so that he could find out how you are doing in your journey of faith,*g* and bring comfort

---

a 3:25 This clause is translated from the Aramaic. The Greek text reads "He who does wrong will receive the consequences for what he has done."

b 4:4 Or "as I should."

c 4:5 The Aramaic could be translated "as you live in the wilderness."

d 4:5 The Aramaic can be translated "sell your last crust of bread," which is a metaphor for making a full commitment (i.e., giving all you've got).

e 4:6 The Aramaic word could also be translated "compassion."

f 4:6 Literally "seasoned with salt." This is an idiom that means "friendly, clear, and making people thirsty for truth."

g 4:7–8 Or "that I may know your affairs."

and encouragement to your hearts. For he is a beloved brother in Christ, a faithful servant of the gospel and my ministry partner in our Master Yahweh's[a] work.

[9]I have also sent Onesimus,[b] who is from your city,[c] and is also a beloved and faithful brother who will inform you of all that we're enduring.

[10-11]Aristarchus, a fellow prisoner here with me, sends you his love. And Joshua (who is also called Justus) along with Mark, the cousin of Barnabas, also send you their loving greetings. You have already been informed that if Mark comes to you, receive him warmly. These three men are the only ones of the circumcision who have aided me here in the work of the kingdom of God, and they have been a great blessing to me.

[12-13]Epaphras, who is also from Colossae, sends his loving greetings. I can tell you that he is a true servant of Christ, who always labors and intercedes for you. His prayers are filled with requests to God that you would grow and mature, standing complete and perfect in the beauty of God's plan for your lives. Epaphras has such great zeal and passion for you and for those who are from Laodicea and from Hierapolis.

[14]And Luke, the beloved physician, sends his warm greetings to you, and Demas also. [15]Give my greetings to all the believers in Laodicea. And pray for dear Nymphas and the church that gathers in her[d] home.

---

a 4:7–8 Again, the Aramaic title for Jesus is Lord (Master) Yahweh; this is the clearest title that could be stated to prove the deity of Jesus Christ.

b 4:9 This was the slave who ran away from his master, Philemon, who was a friend to the apostle Paul. See Philem. 10–12.

c 4:9 Or "he is one of you."

d 4:15 There is some debate about the gender of Nymphas. It may be that many of those who translated this in the early church had difficulty with a church being led by a woman. There are some manuscripts in Greek that have "the church that meets in *her* house."

[16]Once you've read this letter publicly to the church, please send it on to the church of the Laodiceans,[a] and make sure you read the letter that I wrote to them. [17]Be sure you give Archippus this message: "Be faithful to complete the ministry you received from our Lord Jesus!"[b]

[18]Now finally, I, Paul, write this with my own handwriting, and I send my loving greetings to you! Remember me in my imprisonment. May the blessings of God's grace overwhelm you!

Love in Christ,
Paul

---

a 4:16 As stated in the introduction to Ephesians, it is most likely that this missing letter to the Laodiceans is, in fact, the letter to the Ephesian church. However, the tradition of the Eastern Church is that the letter to the Laodiceans was actually 1 and 2 Thessalonians.

b 4:17 It is believed that Archippus was a spiritual leader in the region of Colossae, perhaps the bishop of Laodicea; he is also mentioned in Philem. 2. We can only speculate why Paul wanted this exhortation to be made to him. Some believe he was a minister of Christ who was discouraged and needed to be exhorted to not abandon his calling.

1 THESSALONIANS

Introduction

AT A GLANCE

Author: The apostle Paul
Audience: The church of Thessalonica
Date: AD 50–51
Type of Literature: A letter
Major Themes: The gospel and faith, pleasing God, and
  the future
Outline:
  Letter Opening — 1:1
  Thanksgiving for Faith — 1:2–10
  Ministry Explained, Thanksgiving Renewed — 2:1–3:13
  Exhortation to Christian Living — 4:1–5:11
  Letter Closing — 5:12–28

ABOUT 1 THESSALONIANS

What a fascinating letter! Full of encouragement and exhortation, 1 Thessalonians will leave you richer in your spiritual life. The apostle Paul brought the gospel to the important city of Thessalonica, with an estimated population of 100,000. Originally named Thermai ("hot springs"), the city was renamed Thessalonica, after Alexander the Great's half sister. The city was home to a Jewish community as well as many cults and false religions.

After leaving Philippi, during his second apostolic journey, Paul and his team arrived at the wealthy city of Thessalonica, the capital of Macedonia. As he preached and taught in the synagogue, many Jews and a large number of God-fearing non-Jews became believers and formed a congregation of Christ-followers. (See Acts 17:4.) But Paul and his companions had to cut short their stay, for their lives were in danger.

Shortly after leaving the city, Paul sent Timothy back to make sure the believers were doing well and living faithfully by the truths of the gospel. When Timothy returned, he informed Paul of the great faith, hope, and love that still burned in their hearts. So he wrote them this letter, about two years after the church had been established, in order to comfort and strengthen their hearts. The Thessalonians had let Paul know that they had questions about the appearing of Christ, so Paul addressed that subject in his letter. This was a young church that needed to hear from Paul.

Many scholars have concluded that 1 Thessalonians is one of the earliest known writings of the apostle Paul (along with the books of Galatians and 2 Thessalonians), which makes it perhaps the oldest Christian writing we have. It is dated back to AD 50–51, only twenty years or so after Jesus was crucified and raised from the dead.

In this deeply personal letter, Paul gives us wise and practical advice on how to live our lives with gratitude, grace, and glory. He speaks to the recipients as their "father" (2:11) and their "mother" (2:7). Eight times he addresses the Thessalonian believers as his beloved "brothers and sisters." He even describes them as his "exhilarating joy" (2:19).

Such a treasure is found in the few pages of this letter!

PURPOSE

Writing as a concerned "father" and longing "mother," Paul coauthored this letter with his fellow missionaries Silas and Timothy, to remind these dear believers in Thessalonica of what they had previously taught them and to reinforce what they already knew. After hastily departing them and finding no way to return, Paul dictated this letter to encourage them to maintain their hope in God by persevering, remaining pure, pursuing God's pleasure, and living in a way that prepared them for Christ's return. This concern is captured at the center of this letter:

Then your hearts will be strengthened in holiness so that you may be flawless and pure before the face of our God and Father at the appearing of our Lord Jesus with all his holy ones. (3:13)

Although Paul was encouraged by the Thessalonians' faith, hope, and love, he was still mindful of their vulnerability. So along with his trusted companions Silas and Timothy, Paul sent them this letter to build their spiritual muscles, help them live faithfully, and encourage them as they waited for Christ's return.

AUTHOR AND AUDIENCE

There is little doubt that Paul the apostle dictated the contents of the letter that was later sent to the Christian community at Thessalonica. In fact, many New Testament scholars consider it to be not only one of Paul's earliest letters but one of the earliest New Testament books. And yet Paul isn't the only author, for the letter opens with this: "From Paul, Silas, and Timothy. We send our greetings to you, the congregation of believers in Thessalonica." Paul and his coworkers jointly spoke into the situation faced by their audience, even though the letter was dictated by Paul.

Paul and Silas had a particularly special bond with the Thessalonians, for they had traveled to this Roman city from Philippi during their second missionary journey, after Paul received a vision of a man pleading with them to come. (See Acts 16:9–10.) During this evangelistic mission, a large number of God-fearing non-Jews, as well as many pagan idol-worshipers, turned to faith in Jesus Christ. Paul wrote these baby Christians and this infant church to encourage them to persevere, remain pure, and prepare for the coming of the Lord.

MAJOR THEMES

Faith and the Gospel, Explained and Personalized. While 1 Thessalonians isn't an apologia for the gospel, like Romans or Galatians, we still discover much about its essence. Paul speaks of it as a power (1:4) and as the Lord's message—a message not derived from the words of men but the very word of God (2:13), which was entrusted to the apostles (2:4). The gospel results in our being chosen and called by God (1:4; 4:7). The key verses of 1 Thessalonians are 1:9–10: "You turned to God from idols to serve the true and living God. And now you eagerly expect his Son from heaven—Jesus, the deliverer, whom he raised from the dead and who rescues us from the coming wrath."

Turning from idolatry and sin, toward God in faith and service, was their response to the gospel message that Paul, Silas, and Timothy preached—the good news that Jesus, our deliverer, rose from the dead, rescues us from God's wrath, and will one day return from heaven. This is reaffirmed near the end of the letter: "For God has not destined us to experience wrath but to possess salvation through our Lord Jesus, the Anointed One. He gave his life for us so that we may share in resurrection life in union with him" (5:9–10). There you have it: God's good news explained!

One of the more striking aspects of this letter is Paul's commendation of the believers' faith and the outworking of it in love and hope (1:3). He goes so far as to say that because of their faith, they had "become an example for all the believers to follow" (1:7). They had received the gospel "wholeheartedly," not as a "fabrication of men but as the word of God" (2:13), resulting in their lives being impacted by the gospel's power. Because of this faith, the Thessalonian believers were persecuted yet remained steadfast (3:7). You get the sense that Paul is inviting us to follow in their steps.

Living to Please God. The theme of living in a way that is worthy of the name "Christian" and in a way that pleases God runs strong through Paul's letters. First Thessalonians is no different. From the start, Paul commends these dear believers for putting their faith into practice (1:3). Yet he goes further, reminding them that as God's holy, set-apart people, they are called to live in a particular way.

First he challenges them "to adopt a lifestyle worthy of God" (2:12). When Paul first evangelized this community, this was part of what he taught them. So he reminds them of these teachings here and makes an appeal: "Keep faithfully growing through our teachings even more and more" (4:1). Why? Because "God's will is for you to be set apart for him in holiness" (4:3).

Finally, he reminds them that they are to live differently because they are different: "For you are all children of the light and children of the day. We don't belong to the night nor to darkness" (5:5). While living to please God can be difficult, especially in a culture that lives the exact opposite, it's something we're called to, something God desires from us.

Hopeful Preparation for the Day of the Lord. Paul wants us to be prepared in hope for the day when Christ returns in full glory. The main portion of Paul's letter is framed by this sense of waiting for, expecting, and being prepared for Christ's return. Paul praised the Thessalonians for eagerly expecting God's Son from heaven to rescue them (1:10). He exhorted them to be prepared for the day when he does return, keeping themselves completely flawless until his appearing.

In between waiting and keeping, Paul encourages the believers that those who have already passed away have not died in vain but died in hope—for God will bring with Christ those who have died in a declaration of victory!

He also wants them, and us, to "stay alert and clear-headed" (5:8) as we wait, for we don't know when it will happen. The Lord's return will come unexpectedly and as a complete surprise (5:2). Yet, though we may have questions about the end, we can be encouraged and encourage one another in the hope that we will "share in resurrection life in union with him" (5:10).

1 THESSALONIANS

Faithfulness to Christ

Paul Gives Thanks for the Thessalonians

1 From Paul, Silas,[a] and Timothy.[b] We send our greetings to you, the congregation[c] of believers in Thessalonica,[d]

---

a 1:1 Or "Silvanus," whom most scholars believe is the Silas mentioned as a prophet in the Jerusalem church and Paul's coworker in Macedonia (Acts 15:22–40; 16:19–40; 17:1–16). The name Silas is the Aramaic form of the Hebrew name Saul. Both Silas and Timothy had been with Paul when he first visited Thessalonica (Acts 17:4, 14). There are only four of Paul's letters in the New Testament in which he does not call himself an apostle (1 and 2 Thessalonians, Philippians, and Philemon), most likely because of the deep relationship he already had with them.

b 1:1 Ministry requires teamwork. Paul saw himself as part of a church-planting team made up of three men with wonderful giftings: Paul, Silas, and Timothy.

c 1:1 The Greek word *ekklēsia* is best translated in this context as "congregation." It means "called-out ones." In Greek culture the *ekklēsia* were members of society who were given the duties of legislating on behalf of a city, similar to a city council. They were both "called out" and "called together" to function as those who have the responsibilities of shaping societal norms and the morality of culture.

d 1:1 Thessalonica was the largest city in Macedonia and may have had a population of 200,000 when Paul wrote this letter.

which is in God the Father and the Lord Jesus Christ.[a] May God's delightful grace[b] and peace rest upon you.[c]

[2]We are grateful to God for your lives[d] and we always pray for you. [3]For we remember before our God and Father how you put your faith into practice, how your love motivates you to serve others, and how unrelenting is your hope-filled patience in our Lord Jesus Christ.[e]

[4]Dear brothers and sisters,[f] you are dearly loved by God and we know that he has chosen you to be his very own.[g] [5]For our gospel came to you not merely in the form of words but in mighty power infused with the Holy Spirit

---

a 1:1 The church is both "in" God the Father and "in" Jesus Christ. The Trinity is making room for the bride.

b 1:1 The usage of *charis* (grace) in ancient classical Greek carries the connotation of something that awakens joy and pleasure. The Greek concept of grace imparts delight, often attached to a strong emotional element. Paul uses the term *grace* as a joyous delight that rests upon the people of God (Thomas F. Torrance, *The Doctrine of Grace in the Apostolic Fathers*, 1–2).

c 1:1 Some manuscripts add "from God our Father and the Lord Jesus Christ."

d 1:2 Starting with v. 2 Paul begins one long and complicated Greek sentence that ends with v. 10.

e 1:3 Paul mentions the three invaluable qualities of a believer's life: faith, love, and hope. The Thessalonians put their faith into practice by turning away from all that was false (v. 9). They demonstrated their motive of love by serving God and others (v. 9). And they lived with undying hope that was centered upon the future appearing of Christ (v. 10).

f 1:4 Although the Greek uses the term *brothers* (*adelphoi*), it is intended to express the group identity of those who follow Christ and not meant to be gender exclusive. Paul uses the term eighteen times in five chapters. First Thessalonians could be called Paul's friendliest letter. He describes himself as a "father" and "mother" to them (2:7, 11) and calls them his "joy" and "trophy" (2:19).

g 1:4 The perfect tense of the verb implies that God loved them in the past and continues to love them in the same way.

and deep conviction.*a* Surely you remember how we lived our lives transparently before you to encourage you.*b*

⁶And you became followers*c* of my example and the Lord's when you received the word with the joy of the Holy Spirit, even though it resulted in tremendous trials and persecution.*d* ⁷Now you have become an example for all the believers to follow throughout the provinces of Greece.*e*

⁸The message of the Lord has sounded out from you not only in Greece, but its echo has been heard in every place where people are hearing about your strong faith. We don't need to brag on you, ⁹for everyone tells the story of the kind of welcome you showed us when we first came to you. And everyone knows how wonderfully you turned to God from idols to serve the true and living God. ¹⁰And now you eagerly expect his Son from heaven—Jesus, the

---

a 1:5 True gospel ministry will be expressed by the word of God and characterized by mighty power, releasing the unmistakable presence of the Holy Spirit, and through sincere conviction of truth will be found in those who present it.

b 1:5 Or "for your sakes" (benefit).

c 1:6 Or "imitators."

d 1:6 True conversion delivers us from many things, but is not an assurance that we will never face painful trials or persecution for our faith.

e 1:7 Or "Macedonia and Achaia." Greece was divided into two provinces: the northern region known as Macedonia and the southern one, Achaia. Thessalonica was located in Macedonia, and Corinth, where Paul wrote this letter, was the leading city of Achaia. Although the believers of Thessalonica were novices, their testimony had spread throughout the region.

deliverer, whom he raised from the dead and who rescues us from the coming wrath.[a]

Godly Character of Jesus' Servants

2 My dear brothers and sisters, it's obvious that our ministry among you has proven to be fruitful.[b] [2]And though we had already suffered greatly in Philippi, where we were shamefully mistreated,[c] we were emboldened *by faith* in our God to fearlessly preach his wonderful gospel to you in spite of incredible opposition.

[3]Our coming alongside you to encourage you was not out of some delusion, or impure motive, or an intention to mislead you, [4]but we have been approved by God to be those who preach the gospel. So our motivation to preach is not pleasing people but pleasing God, who thoroughly examines our hearts. [5]God is our witness that when we came to encourage you, we never once used cunning compliments as a pretext for greed, [6]nor did we crave the praises of men, whether you or others.[d] [7]Even though we could have imposed upon you our demands as apostles of

---

a 1:10 The gospel of power will change lives. The Thessalonians had renounced the worship of false gods and turned wholeheartedly to the true God and become faithful servants. Every time true conversion (repentance) takes place, a life is changed. The Thessalonians were famous for these four things: (1) They turned wholeheartedly to God. (2) They abandoned worshiping false gods (idols). (3) They became passionate servants of Christ. (4) They were eagerly anticipating the heavenly Son, Jesus.

b 2:1 Or "Our coming to you has not been in vain" (empty). See Acts 17:1–9.

c 2:2 Paul and Silas had been beaten and imprisoned in Philippi. See Acts 16:11–17:1.

d 2:6 Paul never watered down his message in preaching the gospel. His fearless courage serves as an example to us today to keep our message uncompromised.

Christ,^a instead we showed you kindness and were gentle among you.^b We cared for you in the same way a nursing mother cares for her own children. ⁸With a mother's love and affectionate attachment to you, we were very happy to share with you not only the gospel of God but also our lives—because you had become so dear to us.^c

⁹Beloved brothers and sisters, surely you remember how hard we labored among you. We worked night and day so that we would not become a burden to you while we preached the wonderful gospel of God. ¹⁰With God as our witness you saw how we lived among you—in holiness, in godly relationships,^d and without fault. ¹¹And you know how affectionately we treated each one of you, like a loving father cares for his own children. ¹²We comforted and encouraged you and challenged you to adopt a lifestyle worthy of God, who invites you into his kingdom and glory.^e

The Faithfulness of the Thessalonians

¹³This is why we continually thank God *for your lives*, because you received our message *wholeheartedly*. You

---

a 2:7 The Aramaic can be translated "Although we could have been honored as apostles of the Messiah." See also 1 Cor. 9:1–18; Philem. 8.

b 2:7 Some reliable manuscripts have "We became like little children (infants) among you."

c 2:8 Or "You had become our beloved." Just a few months before, the Thessalonians were complete strangers to Paul. Now he states how dear they had become to his heart. True ministry is caring for others with a father's love and a mother's love—not exerting control or abusive authority over those whom we serve.

d 2:10 Or "righteousness." The Hebraic concept of righteousness extends toward our relationships and how we treat others. Paul stated that he lived in holiness toward God and purity in his relationships with others, so that no one could blame him for wrongdoing.

e 2:12 Our calling is a summons from God to enter into his glory. A possible hendiadys, "his own glorious kingdom."

embraced it not as the fabrication of men but as the word of God. And the word continues to be an energizing force in you who believe.

[14]*My dear* brothers and sisters, the same thing happened to you as happened to God's churches in Christ Jesus that are in Judea. For you received the same kind of mistreatment from your fellow countrymen as they did from theirs, the Jews [15]who killed both the Lord Jesus and the prophets and ran us out of town. They are offending God and hostile to everyone else [16]by hindering us from speaking to the unbelievers[a] so that they might be saved. By so doing they are constantly filling up to the brim the measure of their guilt,[b] and punishment[c] has come upon them at last![d]

Paul's Concern for the Thessalonians

[17]Beloved friends, we may have been torn away[e] from you physically for a season, but never in our hearts. For we have had intense longings and have endeavored to come and see in your faces the reflection of this great love.[f] [18]We *miss you badly*, and I personally wanted to come to you, trying again and again, but our adversary,[g] Satan,

a 2:16 Or "the gentiles."

b 2:16 That is, they are filling up to the limit of their sins before God.

c 2:16 Or "wrath," a metonymy for the punishment resulting from their sins.

d 2:16 Or "completely" (to a full extent). This could be a prophetic word from Paul regarding the soon destruction of Jerusalem in the Roman war of AD 67–70. Paul is not referring to all Jews, for many had become converts and made up the early church. God rejected the empty rituals of Judaism but not the Jewish people. See Rom. 9–11.

e 2:17 Or "We have been [like] orphans."

f 2:17 As translated from the Aramaic. How poetic are the Semitic languages!

g 2:18 The Greek word *satanas* means "adversary," "accuser," "opposer," and it is the title for Satan. In some way Satan worked to hinder Paul from returning to Thessalonica, possibly through the Jews who opposed him.

blocked our way. [19]For what will be our *confident* hope, our *exhilarating* joy, or our *wonderful* trophy[a] that we will boast in before our Lord Jesus at his appearing?[b] It is you! [20]Yes, you are our glorious *pride and* joy![c]

Timothy's Mission

3 When we could bear it no longer, we decided that we would remain in Athens [2]and send Timothy *in our place.*[d] He is our beloved brother and coworker with God[e] in preaching the gospel. *We knew* he would strengthen your faith and encourage your hearts [3]so that no one would be shaken by these persecutions, for you know that we are destined for this.[f] [4]In fact, when we were with you we forewarned you: "Suffering and persecution is coming." And so it has happened, as you well know. [5]For this reason, when I could endure it no longer, I sent *our brother* to find out if your faith was still strong, for I was concerned that the tempter[g] had somehow enticed you and our labor would have been in vain.

[6]But now, Timothy has just returned to us and brought us the terrific news of your faith and love. He informed

---

a 2:19 Or "crown of boasting."

b 2:19 This is the Greek word *parousia,* which can be translated "coming" or "appearing." Paul uses it six times in his letters to the Thessalonians (3:13; 4:15; 5:23; 2 Thess. 2:1, 8).

c 2:20 The true reward of ministry is not money or fame but the souls of men and women we can influence for the glory of God.

d 3:2 This may have been when Paul sent the letter of 2 Thessalonians with Timothy, which would make it earlier than 1 Thessalonians.

e 3:2 Some manuscripts have "servant of God."

f 3:3 That is, the sufferings of persecution are included in God's destined purpose for those who love God and faithfully follow Christ. See Acts 14:22.

g 3:5 Or "harasser," an obvious title for Satan, our adversary.

us that you still hold us dear in your hearts and that you long to see us as much as we long to see you. [7]So, our dear brothers and sisters, in the midst of all our distress and difficulties, your steadfastness of faith has greatly encouraged our hearts. [8]We feel alive again as long as we know that you are standing firm in the Lord.

[9]How could we ever thank God enough for all the wonderful joy that we feel before our God because of you? [10]Every night and day we sincerely and fervently pray that we may see you face-to-face and furnish you with whatever may be lacking in your faith.

[11]Now may our Father God and our precious Lord Jesus[a] guide our steps on a path straight back to you. [12]And may the Lord increase your love until it overflows[b] toward one another and for all people, just as our love overflows toward you. [13]Then your hearts will be strengthened[c] in holiness so that you may be flawless and pure before *the face of* our God and Father at the appearing of our Lord Jesus with all his holy ones.[d] Amen!

Holiness and Love

4 And now, *beloved* brothers and sisters, since you have been mentored by us with respect to living for God and pleasing him, I appeal to you in the name of the Lord Jesus with this request: keep faithfully growing through our teachings even more and more. [2]For you already know the instructions we've shared with you through the Lord Jesus.

---

a 3:11 Some manuscripts add "the Anointed One."

b 3:12 Or "May the Lord make you increase and your love superabound."

c 3:13 The Aramaic can be translated "He will lift up your hearts without contention."

d 3:13 Or "at the coming of the Lord of us, Jesus Christ, with all of the holy myriads of himself."

³God's will is for you to be set apart for him in holiness and that you keep yourselves *unpolluted* from sexual defilement. ⁴Yes, each of you must guard your sexual purity*ᵃ* with holiness and dignity, ⁵not yielding to lustful passions like those who don't know God. ⁶Never take selfish advantage*ᵇ* of a brother or sister in this matter, for we've already told you and solemnly warned you that the Lord is the avenger in all these things. ⁷For God's call on our lives is not to a life of *compromise and* perversion but to a life surrounded in holiness. ⁸Therefore, whoever rejects this instruction isn't rejecting human authority but God himself, who gives*ᶜ* *us his precious gift*—his Spirit of holiness.

Loving Others

⁹There's no need for anyone to say much to you about loving your fellow believers, for God is continually teaching you to unselfishly love one another.*ᵈ* ¹⁰Indeed, your love is what you're known for throughout Macedonia. We urge you, beloved ones, to let this unselfish love increase *and flow through you* more and more. ¹¹Aspire*ᵉ* to lead a calm and peaceful life as you mind your own business*ᶠ*

---

a 4:4 Or "Each of you must possess your vessel equipment." Some see the "equipment" as a wife, but in the context it is sexual purity, not marriage, that is in view. The "vessel" is our body, including sexual urges that must be kept pure and holy with self-respect.

b 4:6 Although technically Paul uses a term for a business transaction, it is more likely, due to the context, a warning about cheating others by enticing them to sexual immorality.

c 4:8 This is in the present tense.

d 4:9 This "God-teaching" (Gr. *theodidaktos*) of divine love came to us through Christ. God taught us to love by his example of giving us his Son.

e 4:11 Or "Make it your driving ambition."

f 4:11 The Aramaic can be translated "Keep your covenants" (promises).

and earn your living, just as we've taught you. [12]By doing this you will live an honorable life, influencing others and commanding respect of even the unbelievers. Then you'll be in need of nothing and not dependent upon others.[a]

The Appearing of the Lord

[13]Beloved brothers and sisters, we want you to be quite certain about the truth concerning those who have passed away,[b] so that you won't be overwhelmed with grief like many others who have no hope. [14]For if we believe that Jesus died and rose again, we also believe that God will bring with Jesus those who died while believing in him.[c] [15]This is the word of the Lord:[d] we who are alive *in him* and remain until the Lord appears will by no means have an advantage over those who have already died,[e] *for both will rise together.*

[16]For the Lord himself will appear with the declaration of victory, the shout of an archangel, and the trumpet blast of God.[f] He will descend from the heavenly realm[g]

---

a 4:12 That is, self-supporting (financially).

b 4:13 Or "about those who have fallen asleep." Paul uses sleep as a euphemism for death.

c 4:14 Or "Through Jesus God will bring with him those who have fallen asleep [died] in Jesus."

d 4:15 This phrase ("the word of the Lord") is used in both the Old and New Testament for inspired prophetic speech. See Gen. 15:1; Isa. 1:10; Jonah 1:1; Luke 22:61; Acts 11:16; 16:32; 19:20. It is possible that this was spoken to Paul in his heavenly encounter, for he had never met the Lord Jesus, and what Paul reveals here is not found in any of the Gospels.

e 4:15 Or "those who have fallen asleep," a euphemism for death.

f 4:16 Or "*in* the declaration . . . *in* the shout . . . and *in* the trumpet blast of God."

g 4:16 Or "The Lord himself will continue habitually descending from heaven within the midst of a declaration of victory, the chief angel's shout, and God's trumpet blast, and the dead in union with Christ will continue raising themselves up first [or one after another]."

and *command* those who are dead in Christ to rise first. [17]Then we who are alive will join them, transported together[a] in clouds[b] to have an encounter[c] with the Lord in the air,[d] and we will be forever joined with the Lord. [18]So encourage one another with these truths.

God's Times and Seasons

5 Now, beloved brothers and sisters, concerning the question of *God's* precise times and specific seasons,[e] you don't need me to write anything to you. [2]For you already know quite well that the day of the Lord[f]

---

a 4:17 Or "caught up together." The Greek word *harpazō* is used as a figure of speech in Greek literature during the time Paul wrote this letter. The book of Enoch and the Dead Sea Scrolls use the same Greek word and imagery to describe spiritual victory, not a "rapture." The word can describe being caught up in the victory of Christ's unveiling. Also, there are Jewish apocalyptic texts that use the same phrasing as Paul's writings but have nothing to do with a physical rapture.

b 4:17 There is no definite article before clouds. It is literally "in clouds." Where the identifying article is missing, it often speaks of quality, or it is used as a descriptive term. The Greek word for "cloud" is often used in the Greek classics of a large body of individuals, and it is so used in this symbolic way in Heb. 12:1–2, speaking of the "great witnesses who encircle us like clouds."

c 4:17 The Greek word *apantēsis* is not a verb (go to meet) but a feminine noun (a meeting or an encounter), and in this context it is the bride of Christ rising to be with Jesus to have an encounter or "[bridal] meeting." This rarely used Greek word is also used in the parable of the ten virgins, referring to the virgins rising up to meet (have a meeting) with the bridegroom. See Matt. 25:1, 6.

d 4:17 This is the Greek word *aer* and is not the sky, but the air around us. See Eph. 2:2 where it is also used not in a literal sense.

e 5:1 That is "the specific intervals of time and the epoch [hinge] periods of time."

f 5:2 See Jer. 30:7; Joel 1:15; 2:1–2; Amos 5:18; Zech. 1:4–18.

will come unexpectedly and as a complete surprise.[a] [3]For while some are saying, "Finally we have peace and security," sudden destruction will arrive at their doorstep, like labor pains seizing a pregnant woman—and with no chance of escape!

[4]But you, beloved brothers and sisters, are not living in the dark, allowing that day to creep up on you like a thief *coming to steal.* [5]For you are all children of the light and children of the day. We don't belong to the night nor to darkness. [6]This is why we must not fall asleep, as the rest do, but keep wide awake and clearheaded. [7]For those who are asleep sleep the night away, and drunkards get drunk at night.[b] [8]But since we belong to the day, we must stay alert and clearheaded by placing the breastplate of faith and love *over our hearts,* and a helmet of the hope of salvation *over our thoughts.*[c] [9]For God has not destined us for wrath but to possess salvation through our Lord Jesus, the Anointed One. [10]He gave his life for us so that we may share in resurrection life[d] in union with him—whether we're awake or asleep. [11]Because of this, encourage the hearts of your fellow believers and support one another, just as you have already been doing.

[12]Dear brothers and sisters, make sure that you show your deep appreciation for those who cherish you and diligently work as ministers among you. For they are your leaders who care for you, teach you, and stand before the Lord on

---

a 5:2 Or "like a thief comes in the night" (as unexpected as a home invasion). See Matt. 24:3–25:46; Mark 13:3–37; Luke 21:5–36; 2 Peter 3:10; Rev. 3:3; 16:15.

b 5:7 See John 3:9–20.

c 5:8 The Aramaic can be translated "be clearheaded in our vision as we are deployed on the battlefield for faithfulness and love, and set apart with the shield of the hope of everlasting life." See Isa. 59:17; Eph. 6:10–17.

d 5:10 As translated from the Aramaic and implied in the Greek.

your behalf. [13]They value you with great love. Because of their service to you, let peace reign among yourselves.[a]

[14]We appeal to you, dear brothers and sisters, to instruct those who are not in their place of battle.[b] *Be skilled at* gently encouraging those who feel themselves inadequate.[c] *Be faithful* to stand your ground. Help the weak to stand again. Be *quick to* demonstrate patience with everyone. [15]Resist revenge, and make sure that no one pays back evil in place of evil but always pursue doing what is beautiful to one another and to all *the unbelievers.*

[16]Let joy be your continual feast.[d] [17]Make your life a prayer. [18]And in the midst of everything be always giving thanks, for this is God's perfect plan for you in Christ Jesus.[e]

---

a 5:13 Verses 12–13 are translated from the Aramaic. The Greek is "Brothers and sisters, we appeal to you to respect [recognize] those who labor among you and have oversight of your lives in the Lord and admonish you. Show them as much respect as possible with great love because of all they do for you. Be at peace among yourselves." Church leaders deserve our financial support and love because of the work they do for our benefit.

b 5:14 Or "those who are disorderly," or "those who are idle." The Greek word *ataktos* is often used for troops that are not in battle formation (unarranged).

c 5:14 Or "those who are losing heart [fainthearted]."

d 5:16 The Aramaic can be translated "Be joyous in every season."

e 5:18 Verses 16–18 identify three areas our lives we must focus on: (1) unbounded joy, (2) praying continually, and (3) giving thanks to God no matter what happens in our lives. These three virtues combine to form the wonderful expression of Christ's life within us.

[19]Never *restrain or* put out the fire of the Holy Spirit.[a] [20]And don't be one who scorns prophecies,[b] [21]but be faithful to examine them by putting them to the test, and afterward hold tightly to what has proven to be right.[c] [22]Avoid every appearance of evil.

[23]Now, may the God of peace and harmony set you apart, making you completely holy. And may your entire being—spirit, soul, and body—be kept completely flawless in the appearing of our Lord Jesus, the Anointed One. [24]The one who calls you by name is trustworthy and will thoroughly complete his work in you.

[25]Now, beloved ones, pray for us.

[26]Greet every brother and sister with a sacred kiss.

[27]I solemnly[d] plead with you before the Lord to make sure that every holy believer among you has the opportunity to hear this letter read to them.

[28]May grace from our Lord Jesus Christ be with you. Amen!

---

a 5:19 See Song. 8:7.

b 5:20 There is an implication in the context of vv. 19–20 that we put out the Spirit's fire when we scorn prophecy. Prophecy is a valid gift of the Holy Spirit needed by the church today. There is no place in Scripture or in church history that indicates the gift of prophecy has ceased or disappeared. It is an active function of the Holy Spirit in the church around the world. We must not ignore, despise, or scorn any true gift of the Holy Spirit. Putting out the fire of the Holy Spirit (v. 19) is connected to scorning the prophetic ministry. We need prophets and prophecy to keep the fire (inspiration) of the Holy Spirit burning in our hearts. See 1 Cor. 12–14.

c 5:21 The Aramaic can be translated "Regard everything seriously and choose what is best."

d 5:27 Or "I put you under oath" (a serious obligation).

2 THESSALONIANS

Introduction

AT A GLANCE

Author: The apostle Paul
Audience: The church of Thessalonica
Date: AD 51
Type of Literature: A letter
Major Themes: Faith, perseverance, justice, Christ's return, laziness, and disunity
Outline:
  Letter Opening — 1:1–2
  Thanksgiving and Prayer — 1:3–12
  The Day of the Lord — 2:1–17
  Idle and Disruptive Believers — 3:1–15
  Letter Closing — 3:16–18

ABOUT 2 THESSALONIANS

What will it be like to live in the last days before Jesus appears? What words of encouragement and warning would God want to give us? Paul's second letter to the Thessalonians gives us some answers. With only forty-seven verses, this book is packed with prophetic insight that will strengthen and prepare us for the coming days. Not only does 2 Thessalonians give us information about what is ahead, it is also a map to guide us through anything that might assail us as we approach the grand finale of all time—the appearing of our Lord Jesus Christ with his glorious messengers of fire!

Although we spend our lives watching and waiting for his appearing, we must live every day for his glory. We are to be alert, awake, and filled with his holiness as we draw closer to the fulfillment of the ages. In this letter we find encouragement for us to stand our ground, be faithful to the end, and always make the message of Christ beautiful by our lives. We must do more than combat evil; we must live for Christ and expect his coming to find us as passionate lovers of God, abandoned to him with all our hearts.

Paul wrote this letter from Corinth around AD 51 (less than a year after writing 1 Thessalonians) to his beloved friends in the city of Thessalonica. They were followers of Jesus who looked to Paul as their apostolic father and were asking him to clarify the events surrounding "the day of the Lord." A faulty understanding of eschatology (the study of the last days) will lead to faulty conduct and even a detachment from our duties in this world. So Paul writes to inspire those who are idle to engage themselves with making a living and presenting the gospel of Christ through the holy example of their changed lives.

We all need the truth of 2 Thessalonians today to keep our lives focused on what is truth as we look to Christ alone to be our strength, no matter how difficult the future may appear. One day we will each be able to personally thank the apostle Paul for writing this inspired letter! May you be blessed as you read 2 Thessalonians.

PURPOSE

Building off of his first letter to the Thessalonian church, which he sent just a year or so prior, Paul gets down to business. It seems the situation had deteriorated in the short time between planting this Christian community along with his coworkers in the gospel and his first letter. So he wrote to encourage them in three main areas: to hold fast to their faith, despite opposition, knowing that God will act on their behalf with promised justice; to live faithfully as they awaited the coming of Jesus in glory; and to confront a group of "busybodies" (3:11) who were burdening and disrupting the life of the community.

Reading this letter, written to this threatened community, will remind us of the gospel's ultimate outcome—the glorious return of Jesus Christ—while helping us remain worthy of our calling by living our faith with conviction every day.

AUTHOR AND AUDIENCE

Although some have suggested 2 Thessalonians was written pseudonymously (written by someone other than Paul, who used Paul's name as his own), there are striking similarities between Paul's first letter and this one. Both contain an extended thanksgiving and a wish prayer, and both close with a prayer of peace. Although this letter lacks the warmth of 1 Thessalonians, it's clear the author already had a personal relationship with his readers. That makes sense if Paul was writing this as a follow-up letter to members of a community he founded, after a short period of time. Given how urgent the situation had become, Paul would have launched straight into his vital words of encouragement and exhortation.

This infant congregation of former pagans in the heart of the eastern region of the Roman Empire was struggling to understand their identity in Christ as well as how to live as God's people in a hostile culture. Knowing they faced a dire situation and confusion about vital issues related to the gospel and Christian discipleship, Paul addressed these dear believers with the care of a spiritual father.

MAJOR THEMES

Perseverance of Faith through Persecution. In his first letter to the Thessalonians, Paul acknowledged the suffering they were experiencing at the hand of a per-secuting culture. He didn't want them to be unsettled by their trials, and he worried that might disrupt the gospel work he began among them and destroy their faith. Now he returns to this theme, praising them for their "unwav-ering faith" and boasting in their "unflinching endur-ance" (1:4) through all of the persecutions and painful trials they had experienced.

We aren't given specifics, but it seems persecution against these believers had ratcheted up significantly, so Paul wanted to encourage them that it wouldn't be in vain. Their perseverance of faith through persecution stands as a model for all the church, one we are urged to follow in endurance, to be counted "worthy of inheriting the kingdom of God" (1:5).

The Promise of God's Justice. In light of their perse-cution and trials, Paul wrote to encourage them that God hadn't forgotten about them. He would act on their behalf by judging their persecutors in the person of Jesus Christ (1:5–2:12).

Consider all that God has promised to do on our behalf to put things right: he will trouble our troublers, giving rest to those who are troubled. "He will bring perfect and full justice to those who don't know God and on those who refuse to embrace the gospel of our Lord Jesus" (1:8). The ungodly will suffer eternal destruction as a just penalty for their wicked ways, being banished from the Lord's presence. All believers will be adorned with glory. With this in mind, "live worthy of all that he has invited you to experience" (1:11).

Confusion about Christ's Coming Clarified. One reason Paul had written the believers in his first letter was to bring clarity as to what happens to believers at death and what will happen when Christ returns. Apparently, that letter didn't lessen their confusion! "Don't you remember that when I was with you I went over all these things?" Paul sarcastically writes. Apparently not! Therefore, Paul unveils further revelation-truth about what we should watch for and expect in these last days as we await the coming of our Lord in full glory.

As we wait, we're exhorted to "stand firm with a masterful grip of the teachings" we've been given, an "eternal comfort and a beautiful hope that cannot fail" (2:15–16).

The Lazy, Unruly, and Undisciplined. One might not expect believers who are lazy and disruptive, undisciplined and unruly, to be called out by Paul in such a short letter, yet they are. There's a reason: they "stray from all that we have taught you" (3:6), becoming a burden to the church. Such people refuse to work—"These people are not busy but busybodies" (3:11). The example of diligent, earnest work that Paul and his companions had set, and the teachings he laid out, were lifted up as a model for these believers. Since they themselves didn't sponge off the church, neither should anyone else. Since they worked hard to provide food and lodging for themselves, so should every believer. Paul's rule still stands: "Anyone who does not want to work for a living should go hungry" (3:10).

2 THESSALONIANS

Living in the Last Days

God's Times and Seasons

1 From Paul, Silas,[a] and Timothy.[b] *We send our greetings* to you, the Thessalonian congregation[c] of believers, which is in God our Father and the Lord Jesus Christ.[d] [2]May God's delightful grace[e] and peace rest upon you.[f]

[3]We feel a personal responsibility to continually be thanking God for you, our spiritual family,[g] every time we pray. And we have every reason to do so because your faith is growing marvelously beyond measure. The unselfish love each of you share for one another is increasing and overflowing! [4]*We point to you as an example of* unwavering faith[h] for all the churches of God. We

---

a 1:1 See the first footnote on 1 Thess. 1:1.

b 1:1 See the second footnote on 1 Thess. 1:1.

c 1:1 See the third footnote on 1 Thess. 1:1.

d 1:1 The church is both "in" God the Father and "in" Jesus Christ. The Trinity is making room for the bride.

e 1:2 The usage of *charis* (grace) in ancient classical Greek carries the connotation of something that awakens joy and pleasure. The Greek concept of grace imparts delight, often attached to a strong emotional element. Paul uses the term *grace* as a joyous delight that rests upon the people of God. See Thomas F. Torrance, *The Doctrine of Grace in the Apostolic Fathers*, 1–2.

f 1:2 Some manuscripts add "from God our Father and the Lord Jesus Christ."

g 1:3 Or "brothers and sisters."

h 1:4 Or "perseverance and faith," a likely hendiadys.

boast about how you continue to demonstrate unflinching endurance*a* through all the persecutions and painful trials you are experiencing.*b* *5*All of this proves that God's judgment is always perfect and is intended to make you worthy of *inheriting* the kingdom of God, which is why you are going through these troubles.

Encouragement of Christ's Appearing

*6*It is right and just for God to trouble your troublers *7*and give rest to the troubled, both to you and to us, at the unveiling*c* of the Lord Jesus from heaven with his messengers of power *8*within a flame of fire. He will bring perfect and full justice to those who don't know God*d* and on those who refuse to embrace the gospel of our Lord Jesus. *9*They will suffer the penalty of eternal destruction, banished from the Lord's presence*e* and from the manifestation of his glorious power.*f* *10*This will happen on that day when he glorifies his holy ones,*g* and they will be marveled at in all those who believed—including you, since in fact, you believed our message.*h*

*11*With this in mind, we constantly pray that our God will empower you to live worthy of all that he has invited

---

a 1:4 The Aramaic can be translated "your hope," making it their faith, their love, and their hope that Paul lauds them for.

b 1:4 No matter what difficulty we may pass through, a growing faith in Christ, an increasing love for others, and unwavering hope will be the keys to coming through it victoriously.

c 1:7 Or "uncovering" or "revelation."

d 1:8 Or "inflicting vengeance upon those who do not know God." See Ps. 79:6; Isa. 66:15; Jer. 10:25.

e 1:9 Or "face."

f 1:9 See Isa. 2:10, 19, 21.

g 1:10 Or "is glorified in his holy ones."

h 1:10 Or "testimony."

you to experience.*ᵃ* And we pray that by his power all
the pleasures of goodness and all works inspired by faith
would fill you completely.*ᵇ* ¹²By doing this the name of
our Lord Jesus will be glorified in you, and you will be
glorified in him, by the *marvelous* grace of our God and
the Lord Jesus Christ.*ᶜ*

The Coming of the Lord

2 Now, regarding the coming*ᵈ* of our Lord Jesus Christ
and our gathering together to him,*ᵉ* we plead with
you, beloved friends, ²not to be easily confused or disturbed in your minds by any kind of spirit, rumor, or letter
allegedly from us, claiming that the day of the Lord*ᶠ* has
already come. ³Don't let anyone deceive you in any way.
Before that day comes the rebellion*ᵍ* must occur and the
"outlaw"*ʰ*—the destructive son—will be revealed *in his true
light.* ⁴He is the opposing counterpart who exalts himself
over everything that is called "God" or is worshiped*ⁱ* and

---

a 1:11 Or "that our God would make you worthy [or considered wor-
thy] of your calling."

b 1:11 This sentence is translated from the Aramaic. The Greek is "By
his power he will fulfill your every resolve for goodness and works
of faith."

c 1:12 Or "our God and Lord, Jesus Christ."

d 2:1 Or "presence."

e 2:1 The noun form of the Greek word for "gathering together" (*epis-
unagoge*) is found twice in the New Testament, here and in Heb.
10:25. It is used as a verb (*episunago*) in Matt. 23:37; 24:31.

f 2:2 This is a common term that describes the day of the Lord's judgment. (See Jer. 30:7; Joel 1:15; 2:1–2; Amos 5:18; Zech. 1:14–18.)

g 2:3 Or "apostasy" or "abandonment" (falling away).

h 2:3 A few manuscripts have "the man who missed the mark" (i.e.,
Adam), while others have "the person owned by [associated with]
lawlessness."

i 2:4 See Dan. 11:36.

who sits enthroned in God's temple^a and makes himself out to be a god.^{b} ^{5}Don't you remember that when I was with you I went over all these things? ^{6}Now you are aware of the ruling power^c so that he may be fully revealed when his time comes. ^{7}For the mystery of lawlessness^d is already active, but the one who prevails^e will do so until he is separated from out of the midst.^{f} ^{8}Then the "outlaw" will be openly revealed, and the Lord will overthrow him by the breath of his mouth^g and bring him to an end^h by the dazzling manifestation of his presence.^{i}

^{9}The presence^j of the "outlaw" is apparent by the activity of Satan, who uses all kinds of *counterfeit* miracles, signs, spurious wonders, ^{10}and every form of evil deception in order to deceive those who are perishing because they rejected the love of the truth^k that would lead them

---

a 2:4 Some see this prophecy fulfilled in AD 70 during the Roman war, when foreigners came into the temple and desecrated it and declared themselves the true rulers of the Jewish people. Roman emperors were considered to be gods. But the one who sits in God's temple, which was not made with hands, is the sin of man, a sinful nature that is traced back to Adam.

b 2:4 See also Ezek. 28:2.

c 2:6 An intransitive verb meaning "to rule" or "to hold sway" or "to possess." The Aramaic likewise is "Now you know that which controls." The neuter form of the Greek participle suggests a principle, not a person, which could be referring to the mystery of lawlessness in human hearts (v. 7). However, some see "it" as the god of this world (Satan) or the Roman Empire, which ruled the world in the days of Paul's writings.

d 2:7 Or "the secret power of lawlessness/wickedness."

e 2:7 Or "restrains."

f 2:7 Or "until he is removed."

g 2:8 Figuratively, this is the word spoken from his mouth, the Word of God. See also Rev. 19:15, 21.

h 2:8 Or "deactivate."

i 2:8 Or "coming."

j 2:9 Or "coming."

k 2:10 Or "did not welcome the love for the truth."

to being saved. [11]Because of this, God sends them a powerful delusion[a] that leads them to believe what is false. [12]So then all who found their pleasure in unrighteousness and did not believe the truth will be judged.

Chosen for Wholeness

[13]We always have to thank God for you, brothers and sisters, for you are *dearly* loved by the Lord. He proved it by choosing you from the beginning for salvation[b] through the Spirit, who set you apart for holiness, and through your belief in the truth.[c] [14]To this end he handpicked you for salvation through the gospel so that you would have[d] the glory of our Lord Jesus Christ.[e]

[15]So then, dear family, stand firm with a masterful grip of the teachings[f] we gave you, either by word of mouth or by our letter.[g]

---

a 2:11 Or "a [power] working of error." The Aramaic can be translated "God will dispatch to them servants of deception."

b 2:13 Or "He has chosen you as firstfruits [in the harvest] for salvation."

c 2:13 Or "by sanctifying your spirits and convincing you of his truth."

d 2:14 Or "share in" or "possess." This is the Greek word *peripoiēsis*, which means "an encompassing," "a surrounding" or "encircling." Believers are brought within the perimeter of the glory of God through Jesus Christ. There is nothing in the context to imply it is a future event, but rather a present enjoyment and participation in the glory of the Lord Jesus Christ (John 17:10, 22).

e 2:14 These two verses (13–14) contain some of the most wonderful truths of the New Testament. Read them over again slowly and think about all that God the Father, God the Son, and God the Spirit have done for us (e.g., his eternal love, the drawing work of the Holy Spirit, sanctification or being set apart for holiness, faith in Jesus, and much more). Paul states in v. 14 that the purpose of our salvation is more than being set free from guilt; it is so that we would share in and possess the glory of Christ (John 17:10, 22).

f 2:15 Or "traditions."

g 2:15 The "letter" Paul refers to is likely 1 Thessalonians.

[16]Now may the Lord Jesus Christ and our Father God, who loved us and in his wonderful grace gave us eternal comfort and a beautiful hope that cannot fail, [17]encourage your hearts and inspire you with strength to always do and speak what is good and beautiful *in his eyes.*[a]

Paul Requests Their Prayers

3 Finally, dear brothers and sisters, pray for us that the Lord's message will continue to spread rapidly and its glory be recognized everywhere, just as it was with you. [2]And pray that God will rescue us from wicked[b] and evil people, for not everyone believes *the message.* [3]But the Lord Yahweh[c] is always faithful[d] to place you on a firm foundation and guard you from the Evil One.[e] [4]We have complete confidence in the Lord concerning you[f] and we are sure that you are doing and will continue to do what we have told you.

[5]Now may the Lord move your hearts into *a greater understanding of* God's pure love for you and into Christ's steadfast endurance.[g]

---

a 2:17 The Aramaic can be translated "He will comfort your hearts and will stand by all [your] words and by all (your) beautiful deeds." Another possible Aramaic translation of this verse is "He will make your hearts a well of prophecy and he will stand you in every word and in every beautiful deed."

b 3:2 The Greek word *atopos* can also be translated "weird," "irrational," "absurd," "disgusting."

c 3:3 As translated from the Aramaic.

d 3:3 Twelve times in the Bible the Lord is described as faithful. (See Deut. 7:9; Isa. 49:7; 1 Cor. 1:9; 10:13; 2 Thess. 3:3; Heb. 10:23; 11:11; 1 Peter 4:19; 1 John 1:9; Rev. 1:5; 3:14; 19:11.)

e 3:3 Or "guard you from evil" (the unproductive and sinful ways of the past).

f 3:4 Or "The Lord gives us confidence in you."

g 3:5 Or "the faithful endurance of [all things] for Christ." Either translation is grammatically possible as a subjective genitive or an objective genitive. The Aramaic can be translated "the hope of the Messiah."

A Warning about Laziness and Disunity

[6]Beloved brothers and sisters, we instruct you, in the name of our Lord Jesus Christ, to stay away from believers who are unruly[a] and who stray from all that we have taught you.[b] [7]For you know very well that you should order your lives after our example, because we were not undisciplined when we were with you. [8]We didn't sponge off of you, but we worked hard night and day to provide our own food and lodging and not be a burden to any of you. [9]It wasn't because we don't have the right to be supported,[c] but we wanted to provide you an example to follow. [10]For when we were with you we instructed you with these words: "Anyone who does not want to work for a living should go hungry."

[11]Now, we hear rumors that some of you are being lazy[d] and neglecting to work—that these people are not busy but busybodies! [12]So with the authority of the Lord Jesus Christ, we order them to go back to work in an orderly

---

a 3:6 Or "undisciplined" or "lazy" or "not in battle order" or "not in your duty station." There is an implication that there were believers who refused to work for a living. Paul is implying that the church should not financially support those who refuse to work. Personal responsibility is a common theme in Paul's teachings.

b 3:6 Or "don't live according to the traditions they received from us."

c 3:9 Those who preach the gospel have the right to be supported financially and deserve their wages (1 Cor. 9:6–18). However, it seems that Paul's custom was to earn his own way when he went into a city for the first time to show the truth of the gospel without mixed motives. His ministry in Thessalonica was somewhat of an anomaly. Because there were believers who were lazy and not working for a living, Paul gave up his right to have financial support from them and chose to work "night and day" (v. 8) to be an example to them.

d 3:11 Or "not showing up for the war" (battle).

fashion and exhort them to earn their own living.[a] [13]Brothers and sisters, don't ever grow weary in doing what is right.[b]

[14]Take special note of anyone who won't obey what we have written and stay away from them, so that they would be ashamed and get turned around.[c] [15]Yet don't regard them as enemies, but caution them as fellow believers.

Conclusion

[16]Now, may the Lord himself, the Lord of peace, pour into you his peace in every circumstance and in every possible way. The Lord's *tangible* presence be with you all.[d]

[17-18]So now, in my own handwriting, I add these words:

Loving greetings to each of you. And may the grace of our Lord Jesus Christ be with you all.

Paul

The above is my signature and the token of authenticity in every letter I write.[e]

---

a 3:12 Or "eat their own bread."

b 3:13 Doing right in this context is not growing tired of honest work. The Hebrew word for "work" (*avodah*) is the same Hebrew word (a homonym) for worship. Our work can be a form of worship. Our lives are to be a seamless expression of offering to God all of our activities as things we do with all our might for the glory of God.

c 3:14 The passive Greek verb *entropē* means "to be turned" (around); that is, to be changed. This was not punishment but an attempt to draw wayward individuals into repentance and bring them back into restored fellowship with the church.

d 3:16 Paul is longing for the guidance, influence, and power that comes from God's presence to be real to them.

e 3:17–18 See 1 Cor. 16:21; Gal. 6:11; Col. 4:18; Philem. 19. The Aramaic ends with "The end of Paul's second letter to the Thessalonians, written from Laodicea [Pisidian]."

1 TIMOTHY

Introduction

AT A GLANCE

Author: The apostle Paul
Audience: Timothy, Paul's spiritual son in the faith
Date: AD 62–63
Type of Literature: A letter
Major Themes: False teachers, false doctrine, church leadership, and God's household
Outline:
  Letter Opening — 1:1–2
  Ordering and Organizing the Church, Part 1 — 1:3–3:16
  Ordering and Organizing the Church, Part 2 — 4:1–6:19
  Letter Closing — 6:20–21

ABOUT 1 TIMOTHY

First and 2 Timothy have been recognized as "Pastoral Epistles"—letters written by Paul for pastors and leaders to help them bring order and ordain elders (pastors) for the churches he planted. In fact, Timothy was an apostolic apprentice to Paul, mentored by a spiritual father who poured into his life, even after being sent out to establish churches and bring them to maturity. Timothy was the extension of Paul's apostolic ministry. Perhaps we should view these two letters more as "Apostolic Epistles" instead of Pastoral Epistles.

One reason we know that Timothy's ministry was unlike the pastoral ministry of today is that Timothy was an itinerant apostle who planted and brought healing and truth to the churches in which he ministered. Some of the locations he ministered in would include Thessalonica (1 Thess. 3:2–6), Corinth (1 Cor. 4:17; 16:10; 2 Cor. 1:19), Philippi (Phil. 2:19–23), Berea (Acts 17:14), and Ephesus (1 Tim. 1:2). His ministry eventually brought him imprisonment, much like his apostolic mentor, Paul (Heb. 13:23).

Timothy's name means "honored by God." He was from the city of Lystra, the place where Paul was stoned to death and then raised from the dead (see Acts 14:19–20). It may have been that Timothy witnessed what happened to Paul and was converted through what he saw. Paul recruited young Timothy and raised him up to take the message of the gospel to the nations. He soon began to travel with Paul in his missionary journeys and was eventually trusted with great responsibilities to teach and instruct the church.

Timothy was the son of a mixed marriage with a Greek father and a Jewish mother, whose name was Eunice ("joyous victory"). His mother was a convert to Christ and was distinguished by her faith. Timothy was likely in his thirties when Paul wrote him this challenging letter.

Timothy's ministry was in more than one location, for he was told to do the "work of an evangelist" in planting churches and winning souls to Christ. He was Paul's faithful representative to the churches of Thessalonica (1 Thess. 3:2), Corinth (1 Cor. 4:17), Philippi (Phil. 2:19), and Ephesus (1 Tim. 1:3)—yet it was in Ephesus where Paul left him to keep watering the seeds that had been planted to help the church there mature.

Paul instructs Timothy about the administration of the church and encourages him to hold up a high standard for those who lead. The qualifications for church leadership are spelled out in 1 Timothy (and Titus). And we are given clear instructions about caring for widows and for supporting the leaders of the church financially. Generally speaking, 1 Timothy could be seen as a manual for church planting. The key verse is found in 3:15: "But if I'm delayed in coming, you'll already have these instructions on how to conduct the affairs of the church of the living God, his very household, the supporting pillar and firm foundation of the truth."

What heavenly principles are revealed in this letter!

PURPOSE

The clear purpose of 1 Timothy is to reveal and emphasize the glorious truths of God. False teachers had begun to infiltrate the church of Ephesus, and Timothy was given the mission of preserving the truth and cleansing the church of error. Good relationships and spiritual growth can only come when the church grows in maturity and knows the difference between truth and error. There are wonderful revelations waiting for us in 1 Timothy that will focus our hearts on Christ, his glory, and his resurrection.

AUTHOR AND AUDIENCE

What beautiful words Paul shares with his spiritual son, Timothy! We are about to overhear the intimate words of encouragement and inspiration that a first-century apostle shared with his protégé. If we have any example at all of mentoring in the Bible, it is seen here in the relationship Paul had with Timothy. Written about AD 62–63, Paul imparts to Timothy the wisdom and revelation that is required to plant churches and lead an entire region into spiritual breakthrough.

MAJOR THEMES

False Teachers and Doctrine. Every generation has seen its fair share of false teaching; ours is no different, and neither was Timothy's. Paul commands him to confront false teachers and oppose unorthodox doctrines that "emphasize nothing more than the empty words of men" (1:6). He exhorts him to maintain his personal faith and warns against falling away, like others.

Qualifications for Church Leaders. In this letter to his ministry coworker, Paul has provided the church throughout the ages a helpful list of qualifications for two offices: overseers/elders and deacons. Both church officers are called to a similar standard of high moral and personal conduct, which includes integrity, peace, temperateness, generosity, and a well-managed household.

The Household of God. Throughout this letter from heaven, Paul explains what it means to live in the household of God. He outlines the proper treatment for widows, and he lays out the expectations for slaves, which can apply to workers too. He even says how the church should disciple its own. Paul gives Timothy the task of teaching Christ's vision for how his household should exist in the world.

1 TIMOTHY

Heaven's Truth

Introduction

1 From Paul, an apostle in Christ Jesus, for it was Jesus himself, our living hope, who sent me as his servant by the command of God, our life-giver.[a]

[2] Timothy, you are my true spiritual son in the faith. May abundant grace, mercy, and total well-being[b] from God the Father and the Anointed One, our Lord Jesus, be yours!

Timothy's Ministry in Ephesus

[3] As I urged you when I left for Macedonia,[c] I'm asking that you remain in Ephesus to instruct them not to teach or follow the error of deceptive doctrines, [4] nor pay any attention to cultural myths, traditions, or the endless study of genealogies.[d] Those digressions only breed controversies and debates. They are devoid of power that builds up and strengthens the church in the faith of God.

[5] For we reach the goal of fulfilling all the commandments when we love others deeply with a pure heart, a

---

a 1:1 Or "Savior."

b 1:2 The Hebrew concept of peace includes health, prosperity, and peace of mind.

c 1:3 As translated from the Aramaic.

d 1:4 The Jewish people have always been diligent to carefully record their genealogies; yet, the reference to genealogies here may also include the apocryphal writings of Jewish mysticism, detailing the origins of angelic beings involved in creation.

clean conscience, and sincere faith. ⁶Some believers have been led astray by teachings and speculations that emphasize nothing more than the empty words of men. ⁷They presume to be expert teachers of the law,ᵃ but they don't have the slightest idea of what they're talking about and they simply love to argue!

Paul's Use of the Law

⁸We know that the moral code of the law is beautiful when applied as God intended, ⁹but actually, the law was not established for righteous people, but to bring conviction of sin to the unrighteous. The law was established to bring the revelation of sin to the evildoers and rebellious, the sinners without God, those who are vicious and perverse, and to those who strike their father or their mother,ᵇ sinners, murderers, ¹⁰rapists, those who are sexually impure, homosexuals,ᶜ kidnappers, liars, those who break their oaths, and all those who oppose the teaching of godliness and purity in the church! *They are the ones the law is for.*

¹¹I have been commissioned to preach the wonderful news of the glory of the exalted God. ¹²My heart spills over with thanks to God for the way he continually empowers me, and to our Lord Jesus, the Anointed One, who found me trustworthy and who authorized me to be his partner in this ministry.

Empowering Mercy

¹³Mercy kissed me, even though I used to be a blasphemer, a persecutor of believers, and a scorner of what turned out to be true. I was ignorant and didn't know

---

a 1:7 Or "Torah."
b 1:9 As translated from the Aramaic. The Greek reads "those who murder their father or murder their mother."
c 1:10 The Aramaic can be translated "molesters of male children."

what I was doing. [14]I was flooded with such incredible grace, *like a river overflowing its banks,*[a] until I was full of faith and love for Jesus, the Anointed One!

[15]I can testify that the Word is true and deserves to be received by all, for Jesus Christ came into the world to bring sinners back to life—even me, the worst sinner of all! [16]Yet I was captured by grace, so that Jesus Christ could display through me the outpouring of his Spirit[b] as a pattern to be seen for all those who would believe[c] in him for eternal life.

[17]Because of this my praises rise to the King of all the universe[d] who is indestructible,[e] invisible, and full of glory, the only God[f] who is worthy of the highest honors throughout all of time and throughout the eternity of eternities! Amen!

Paul Encourages Timothy to Remain Faithful

[18-19]So Timothy, my son, I am entrusting you with this responsibility, in keeping with the very first prophecies that were spoken over your life, and are now in the process of fulfillment in this great work of ministry, in keeping with the prophecies spoken over you. With this encouragement *use your prophecies* as weapons as you wage spiritual warfare by faith and with a clean conscience. For there are many who reject these virtues and

---

a 1:14 Paul uses the Greek word *pleonazō*, which means "super-abounding grace."

b 1:16 As translated from the Aramaic. The Greek text reads "that Jesus would demonstrate his perfect patience."

c 1:16 Or "destined to believe."

d 1:17 Or "King of the ages."

e 1:17 The Aramaic word used here is a direct reference to the physical body of Christ that did not decompose in the tomb, but was raised in resurrection.

f 1:17 As translated from the Aramaic. Some Greek texts have "the only wise God."

are now destitute of the true faith, [20]such as Hymenaeus[a] and Alexander[b] who have fallen away. I have delivered them both over to Satan to be rid of them and to teach them to no longer blaspheme!

Instruction on Prayer

2 Most of all, I'm writing to encourage you to pray with gratitude to God. Pray for all men with all forms of prayers and requests as you intercede with intense passion. [2]And pray for every political leader[c] and representative,[d] so that we would be able to live tranquil, undisturbed lives, as we worship the awe-inspiring God with pure hearts. [3]It is pleasing to our Savior-God *to pray for them.* [4]He longs for everyone to embrace his life and return to the full knowledge of the truth.

[5]For God is one, and there is one Mediator between God and the sons of men—the true man, Jesus, the Anointed One. [6]He gave himself as ransom-payment for everyone. Now is the proper time for God to give the world this witness. [7]I have been divinely called as an apostle to preach this revelation, which is the truth. God has called me to be a trustworthy teacher to the nations.

---

a 1:20 The name Hymenaeus is also the name of the pagan god of the bridal song sung by the attendants of the bride during the ceremony. He was invoked by the bride's friends in hope that he would come and manifest himself. Perhaps Hymenaeus was attempting to mix the worship of false gods into the church. See also 2 Tim. 2:17.

b 1:20 Alexander's name means "protector of men," or "man pleaser." When the church attempts to please men, we can quickly fail to please God.

c 2:2 Or "kings."

d 2:2 Or "magistrates."

[8]Therefore, I encourage the men to pray on every occasion[a] with hands lifted to God in worship with clean hearts, free from frustration or strife.[b]

Conduct of Women

[9]And that the women *would also pray*[c] with clean hearts, dressed appropriately and adorned modestly and sensibly, not flaunting their wealth.[d] [10]But *they should be recognized* instead by their beautiful deeds of kindness, suitable as one who worships God.

[11]Let the women *who are new converts*[e] be willing to learn with all submission to their leaders and not speak out of turn.[f] [12]I don't advocate that the *newly converted*[g]

---

a 2:8 Or "wherever you pray."

b 2:8 Or "anger or scheming."

c 2:9 Prayer is implied, but made explicit from the context of v. 8.

d 2:9 Literally "not with braids of gold, or with pearls, or gorgeous robes."

e 2:11 Implied and understood by the cultural context of that day.

f 2:11 Literally "quietly." In the context of that day, it referred to women arguing with their male congregational leaders. In the temple worship of Diana, the goddess of the Ephesian people, it was most common to have female leadership. For the women who converted to Christ, their only cultural context of worship was that the women were the leaders. In the church, however, it was the men who more commonly made up the leadership of the congregations. Paul telling the women to "be willing to learn" means he was instructing them to take a respectful posture of a disciple in this new way of worshiping the true God. When Paul instructs them not to be teachers, he was apparently referring to their old religious system where it was the women who were the temple leaders and teachers of their goddess religion in Ephesus. This entire passage from 1 Tim. 2:9–15 is arguably one of the more difficult texts to translate in Paul's writings, and has a number of plausible translations and interpretations. However, this translation has chosen to make clear what was implicitly understood by the early Christians in Ephesus, making it explicit for those of us from another culture and another era.

g 2:12 Implied and understood by the cultural context of that day.

women be the teachers in the church, assuming authority over the men, but to live in peace. [13]For God formed
Adam first,[a] then Eve. [14]Adam did not mislead Eve, but
Eve misled him and violated the command of God.[b] [15]Yet
salvation will come through a child born by a woman,
and women will be saved by that "child" if they continue
in faith with love, holiness, and self-control.[c]

Leaders in the Church

3 If any of you[d] aspires to be an overseer[e] in the church;
you have set your heart toward a noble ambition, for
the word is true! [2]Yet an elder needs to be one who is
without blame before others.

He should be one whose heart is for his wife alone *and
not another woman.*[f] He should be recognized as one who
is sensible, and well-behaved, and living a disciplined

---

a 2:13 One of the prevailing Gnostic heresies of that era was that Eve
was formed first, then Adam. Paul puts that debate to rest with this
verse.

b 2:14 As translated from the Aramaic. The Greek says "Adam was not
deceived but the woman was beguiled and has come into transgression."

c 2:15 Some have interpreted the Greek text to imply that it was Mary
who gave birth to Jesus and that he is the Child that saves us all and
redeems womanhood. This Messianic interpretation can be found in
some modern (Ellicott, Lock, Oden, von Soden, Wohlenberg) as well
as ancient commentators (Ignatius, Eph., 19; Irenaeus, Haer., III.22,
V.19; Justin, Dial., 100; Tertullian, De Car., XLCI, 17). See also Gen.
3:15; Gal. 4:4.

d 3:1 Some translations have "men," however, the Greek word is not
gender specific.

e 3:1 There are a number of terms that are synonymous for elder, such
as: pastor, shepherd, presbyter, bishop, overseer, or guardian. These
all describe the one office of pastor mentioned in Eph. 4:11.

f 3:2 This literally means "a one-woman kind of man" or "faithful
to your woman [wife]," which implies much more than simply not
being a polygamist. It was culturally common for men to have more
than one wife or concubines in that era.

life. He should be a "spiritual shepherd" who has the gift of teaching,[a] and is known for his hospitality.

[3]He cannot be a drunkard, or someone who lashes out at others,[b] or argumentative, or someone who simply craves more money,[c] but instead, recognized by his gentleness.

[4]His heart should be set on guiding his household with wisdom and dignity;[d] bringing up his children to worship with devotion and purity. [5]For if he's unable to properly lead his own household well, how could he properly lead God's household?

[6]He should not be a new disciple[e] who would be vulnerable to living in the clouds of conceit and fall into pride, making him easy prey for Satan.[f] [7]He should be respected by those who are unbelievers, having a beautiful testimony among them[g] so that he will not fall into the traps of Satan and be disgraced.

[8]And in the same way the deacons[h] must be those who are pure and true to their word, not addicted to wine, or with greedy eyes on the contributions.[i] [9]Instead, they must faithfully embrace the mysteries of faith while keeping a clean conscience. [10]And each of them must be found

---

a 3:2 Or "able to teach."

b 3:3 The Aramaic can be translated "not swift to strike."

c 3:3 The Aramaic can be translated "merciful to money." Some see in this the concept of not showing favoritism because of someone's economic status.

d 3:4 Literally "beautifully."

e 3:6 The Aramaic can be translated "a new plant," which implies shallow roots.

f 3:6 The Greek literally means "fall into Satan's court of law."

g 3:7 As translated from the Greek. The Aramaic uses a metaphor, "a beautiful testimony from the wilderness." This means he has passed through his wilderness journey and is now seen as tested and proven.

h 3:8 The Aramaic can be translated "ministers."

i 3:8 Or "corrupt profits."

trustworthy according to these standards before they are given the responsibility to minister as servant-leaders without blame.

[11]And the women[a] also who serve the church should be dignified,[b] faithful in all things,[c] having their thoughts set on truth, and not known as those who gossip.

[12]A deacon's heart must be toward his wife alone, leading his children and household with excellence. [13]For those who serve in this way will obtain an honorable reputation[d] for themselves and a greater right to speak boldly in the faith that comes from Jesus Christ!

[14]I'm writing all this with the expectation of seeing you soon. [15]But if I'm delayed in coming, you'll already have these instructions on how to conduct the affairs of the church of the living God, his very household and the supporting pillar and firm foundation of the truth.

The Mystery of Righteousness
[16]For the mystery of righteousness is beyond all
    question![e]
He was revealed as a human being,

---

a 3:11 The word used here can mean "women" or "wives." This may refer to women deacons. Phoebe is called a deacon in Rom. 16:1.

b 3:11 As translated from the Greek, the Aramaic can be translated "modest."

c 3:11 Or "temperate."

d 3:13 Or "a good rank."

e 3:16 This is the only place where this phrase occurs in the New Testament. The "mystery of righteousness" (godliness) is Jesus Christ living within the believer. The word *mystery* (secret) is found twenty-seven times in the New Testament. We "must faithfully embrace the mysteries of our faith while keeping a clean conscience" (v. 9). Although Paul did speak Greek, his native language was Aramaic, which is difficult to translate into Greek. The Aramaic word used here for mysteries is ʿarza. This is the Aramaic word for a cedar tree. A cedar tree has deep, firm roots. So must our faith be rooted inside these mysteries.

and as our great High Priest in the Spirit!*
Angels gazed upon him *as a man*
  and the glorious message of his kingly rulership
  is being preached to the nations!
Many have believed in him
  and he has been taken back to heaven,
  and has ascended into the place of exalted glory
  in the heavenly realm.
Yes, great is this mystery of righteousness!

Warning against False Teachers

4 The Holy Spirit has explicitly revealed:* At the end of this age, many will depart from the true faith one after

---

a 3:16 As translated by the implication of the Aramaic. The Greek says, "justified in the Spirit." Although some interpret it to mean his resurrection, that seems indefinite and with little meaning to today's reader. There is deep and beautiful poetic artistry here in this passage. The word order of the Aramaic lines is convincing that glorious and hidden truths are tucked into these verses; they are full of Jewish word plays and symbolism and read like a poem. Many have concluded that this passage was an ancient hymn sung by the early church. Two different Aramaic words for "righteousness" are used in v. 16. The first word is *kanota* which is clearly connected to the word for "priest" or *kahna*. An Aramaic or Hebrew reader would clearly connect this "righteousness" to the priestly ministry. In poetic and perhaps subtle linguistic form, this points us to the High Priest of our faith. The second word used that is most often translated "righteousness" is *atzaddaq*; the word in the line before used for messenger (angels) is *malaka*, which is a form of the word for king (*malak*). To summarize, you have the words "great [high] priest," "king," and "righteousness," which is the name for Melchizedek, (King of Righteousness). Truly, this mystery of righteousness is great!

b 4:1 The Greek text could be translated "the Spirit says publicly." This is most likely through prophetic utterance in the church. God's Spirit still speaks to his people today through gifts of prophecy, tongues and interpretation of tongues, and in many other forms. Paul is likely quoting a prophecy.

another, devoting themselves to spirits[a] of deception and following demon-inspired revelations and theories. [2]Hypocritical liars[b] will deceive many, and their consciences won't bother them at all! [3]They will require celibacy and dietary restrictions that God doesn't expect, for he created all foods to be received with the celebration of faith by those who fully know the truth. [4]We know that all creation is beautiful to God and there is nothing to be refused if it is received with gratitude. [5]All that we eat is made sacred by the Word of God and prayer.

[6]If you will teach the believers these things, you will be known as a faithful and good minister of Jesus, the Anointed One. Nurture others in the living words of faith and in the knowledge of grace which you were taught.

[7]Be quick to abstain from senseless traditions[c] and legends,[d] but instead be engaged in the training of truth that brings righteousness.

Conduct of God's Servants

[8]For athletic training only benefits you for a short season, but righteousness brings lasting benefit in everything; for righteousness contains the promise of life, for time and eternity. [9]Faithful is the Word, and everyone should accept him![e]

[10]For the sake of this ministry, we toil tirelessly and are criticized continually,[f] simply because our hope is in the

---

a 4:1 Aramaic and Hebrew speakers would view this as an idiom for "deceiving prophecies."

b 4:2 The Aramaic can be translated "they will seduce with false appearances."

c 4:7 Or "fables."

d 4:7 Or "the fiction of old wives' tales."

e 4:9 As translated from the Aramaic. The Greek text reads "this is a faithful saying and is worthy to be fully accepted."

f 4:10 As translated from the Aramaic. In place of "criticized continually" the Greek text has "contend for the [athletic] prize."

living God. He is the wonderful life-giver[a] of all the children of men, and even more so to those who believe.

[11]Instruct and teach the people all that I've taught you. [12]And don't be intimidated by those who are older than you; simply be the example they need to see by being faithful and true in all that you do. Speak the truth[b] and live a life of purity and authentic love as you remain strong in your faith.

[13]So until I come, be diligent in devouring the Word of God, be faithful in prayer, and in teaching the believers.

[14]Don't minimize the powerful gift that operates in your life, for it was imparted to you by the laying on of hands of the elders and was activated through the prophecy they spoke over you. [15]Make all of this your constant meditation and make it real with your life so everyone can see that you are moving forward. [16]Give careful attention to your spiritual life and every cherished truth you teach, for living what you preach will release salvation inside you and to all those who listen to you.

Conduct toward Others

5 Don't be harsh or verbally abusive to an older man;[c] it is better to appeal to him as a father. And as you minister to the younger men it is best to encourage them as your dear brothers. [2]Honor the older women[d] as mothers, and the younger women, treat as your dear sisters with utmost purity.[e]

[3]The church needs to honor and support the widows, especially those who are in dire need. [4]But if they have children or grandchildren at home, then it is only proper to let

---

a 4:10 As translated from the Aramaic. The Greek word is "Savior."
b 4:12 As translated from the Greek.
c 5:1 Or "elder" (one who is given responsibility within the church).
d 5:2 Or "woman elders."
e 5:2 Or "holiness."

them provide for the ones who raised them when they were children, for kindness begins at home and it pleases God.

[5]For the true widow[a] is all alone and has placed her complete hope in God. She is Messiah's missionary[b] *and will need the support of the church* as one who remains in prayer day and night. [6]But the widow who serves only herself lives a life of self-indulgence and is wasting her life away.

[7]Be sure to give clear instruction concerning these matters so that none of them will live with shame. [8]For if a believer fails to provide for their own relatives when they are in need, they have compromised[c] their convictions of faith *and need to be corrected*, for they are living worse than the unbelievers.

[9]The widows who are worthy to be supported by the church should be at least sixty years old and not remarried. [10]They should have a beautiful testimony of raising their families, practicing hospitality, encouraging other believers, comforting troubled ones,[d] and have a reputation for doing good works.

[11]But you need not concern yourself with the younger widows, for some will depart from the Messiah because of their desire to remarry.[e] [12]For they will face their own punishment[f] of living with a disturbed conscience for invalidating their former faith. [13]Those widows who go around from house to house as busybodies[g] are only

---

a 5:5 There is an implication in the Aramaic that the "true widow" is one whose husband was killed due to persecution of believers.

b 5:5 As translated from the Aramaic.

c 5:8 Or "denied."

d 5:10 Or "paying the expenses of those who are persecuted."

e 5:11 There is a sexual connotation implied in the text.

f 5:12 Or "judgment."

g 5:13 The Greek word used for "busybodies" can also imply "gaining illegal knowledge of the supernatural." See Acts 19:19 where the same Greek word is used for black magic.

learning to be lazy, making their situation even worse by talking too much, gossiping, and speaking things they shouldn't. They become far too obsessed with empty things that will not bear good fruit.

[14]For this reason, teach the younger women to remarry and bear children and care for their household. This will keep them from giving our adversary a reason to gloat. [15]For there are already those who have begun to turn aside from their faith and are influenced by Satan.

[16]So if any believer has a widow in their family, instruct them to support her financially so that the church will not be burdened with her care. This will leave finances available for those widows who are truly in need.

Respect toward Church Leaders

[17]The pastors[a] who lead the church well should be paid well. They should receive double honor for faithfully preaching and teaching the revelation of the Word of God. [18]For the Scriptures have taught us: "Do not muzzle an ox or forbid it to eat while it grinds the grain."[b] And also, "The one who labors deserves his wages."[c]

[19]Refuse to listen to suspicious accusations against the pastors who lead the flock unless you have two or three witnesses to confirm the accusations. [20]But if indeed you find that they have sinned, bring correction to them before the congregation so that the rest of the people will respect you.[d]

[21]Timothy, in the presence of God and our Lord Jesus Christ, and before the chosen messengers,[e] I solemnly

---

a 5:17 Or "elders," also v. 19.

b 5:18 See Deut. 25:4.

c 5:18 See Lev. 19:13; Deut. 24:15.

d 5:20 Or "fear." That is, the congregation will see proper correction and fear falling into sin.

e 5:21 This word can refer to angels or men.

charge you to put into practice all these matters without bias, prejudice, or favoritism.

[22]Don't be hasty to ordain them with the laying on of hands, or you may end up sharing in their guilt should they fall. Keep yourself pure and holy with your standards high. [23](If drinking the water causes you to have stomach ailments,[a] drink some wine instead.)

[24]The sins of some people stand out and are well known. Yet there are others whose sins are not as obvious, but the truth of who they really are will eventually be seen and will bring them judgment.[b] [25]It is the same way with good works, even if they are not known at first, they will eventually be recognized and acknowledged.

6 Instruct every employee[c] to respect and honor their employers,[d] for this attitude presents to them a clear testimony of God's truth and renown. Tell them to never provide them with a reason to discredit God's name because of their actions. [2]Especially honor and respect employers who are believers and don't despise them, but serve them even more, for they are fellow believers. They should be at peace with them as beloved members of

---

a 5:23 The Greek text literally means "bladder frequency." This translation has chosen to bracket this parenthetical verse to show it is inserted in the middle of Paul's words regarding the topic of ordination (laying on of hands). Paul does not encourage the drinking of wine, nor does he condemn its moderate use.

b 5:24 An alternate Aramaic translation is "there are some who confess their sins and bring them [their sins] to judgment, and there are those whose sins follow them."

c 6:1 Or "those under the yoke of performance" (servitude or slavery). The Greek text clearly refers to slaves and masters, but the Aramaic is somewhat ambiguous and could still be referring to the topic of ch. 5. "Those" would refer to the leadership of the church instead— pastors, deacons, and deaconesses.

d 6:1 Or "masters," also in v. 2.

God's family. Be faithful to teach them these things as their sacred obligation.

False Teachers and True Riches

³But if anyone spreads false teaching that does not agree with the healthy instruction of our Lord Jesus, teaching others that holy awe of God[a] is not important, then they prove they know nothing at all! It's obvious they don't value or hold dear the healing words of our Lord Jesus Christ. ⁴They are covered with the clouds of conceit. They are loaded[b] with controversy, and they love to argue their opinions and split hairs. The fruit of their ministry is contention, competition, and evil suspicions.

⁵They add misery to many lives by corrupting their minds and cheating them of the truth. They equate the worship of God with making great sums of money.[c]

⁶We have a "profit" that is greater than theirs—our holy awe of God! To have merely our necessities is to have enough.

⁷Isn't it true that our hands were empty when we came into the world, and when we leave this world our hands will be empty again?

⁸Because of this, food and clothing is enough to make us content.

⁹But those who crave the wealth of this world slip into spiritual snares. They become trapped by the troubles that

---

a 6:3 The Aramaic here and in v. 6 literally means "the doctrine of the fear of God." The fear of God is one of the seven spirits of God, the spirit of the fear of God (Isa. 11:2–3). To teach there is no fear of God would be leading people away from the Holy Spirit. The fear of God is more than simply loving and respecting God. There are over one hundred references in both the Old and New Testaments that speak of "the fear of God."

b 6:4 The Aramaic can be translated "sick with controversy."

c 6:5 Or "to be godly is the way to get rich."

come through their foolish and harmful desires, driven by greed and drowning in their own sinful pleasures. And they take others down with them into their corruption and eventual destruction.

[10]Loving money[a] is a root of all evils. Some people run after it so much that they have given up their faith. Craving more money pushes them away from the faith into error, compounding misery in their lives!

Paul's Final Exhortation to Timothy

[11]Timothy, you are God's man, so run from all these errors. Instead, chase after true holiness, justice, faithfulness, love, hope,[b] and tender humility. [12]So fight with faith for the winner's prize! Lay your hands upon eternal life, to which you were called and about which you made the good confession before the multitude of witnesses![c]

[13]So now, I instruct you before the God of resurrection life[d] and before Jesus, the Anointed One, who demonstrated a beautiful testimony even before Pontius Pilate, [14]that you follow this commission faithfully with a clear conscience[e] and without blemish until the appearing of our Lord Jesus Christ.

[15]Yes, God will make his appearing in his own divine timing,[f] for he is the exalted God, the only powerful One, the King over every king, and the Lord of power! [16]He alone is the immortal God,[g] living in the unapproachable light of divine glory! No one has ever seen his fullness, nor can

---

a 6:10 Or "insatiable greed for money."

b 6:11 Or "patience."

c 6:12 As translated from the Aramaic.

d 6:13 Or "the God who resurrects all."

e 6:14 Or "without defilement."

f 6:15 By implication, the second coming of Jesus.

g 6:16 Or "incorruptible God."

they, for all the glory and endless authority of the universe belongs to him, forever and ever. Amen!

[17]To all the rich of this world, I command you not to be wrapped in thoughts of pride over your prosperity, or rely on your wealth, for your riches are unreliable and nothing compared to the living God. Trust instead in the one who lavishes upon us all good things, fulfilling our every need.[a]

[18]Remind the wealthy to be rich in remarkable works of extravagant generosity, willing to share with others. [19]These spiritual investments will provide a beautiful foundation for their lives and secure for them a great future, as they lay their hands upon the meaning of true life.

[20]So, my son Timothy,[b] don't forget all that has been deposited within you. Escape from the empty echoes of men[c] and the perversion of twisted reasoning.[d] [21]For those who claim to possess this so-called knowledge have already wandered from the true faith.

May God's grace empower you always!

Love in Christ,
Paul

---

a 6:17 Or "pleasure."

b 6:20 Paul uses an endearing variation of Timothy's name; it could almost be read "Oh Timmy." This translation includes the words, *my son*, to make this explicit.

c 6:20 This is an Aramaic figure of speech that means literally "daughters of the voice [echoes] of vanity." The Greek text reads "profane and vain babblings."

d 6:20 As translated from the Aramaic, which also means, "false doctrines." The Greek is "false [so-called] science."

2 TIMOTHY

Introduction

AT A GLANCE

Author: The apostle Paul
Audience: Timothy, Paul's spiritual son in the faith
Date: AD 65–67
Type of Literature: A letter
Major Themes: False teachers, false doctrine, suffering, perseverance, and faithfulness
Outline:
Letter Opening — 1:1–2
Thanksgiving for Timothy's Faith — 1:3–5
Encouragement to Timothy — 1:6–2:13
Instructions for Timothy — 2:14–4:8
Letter Closing — 4:9–22

ABOUT 2 TIMOTHY

This could be called the last will and testament of Paul the apostle. Filled with warnings of the troubles that were ahead, this letter speaks to our generation with an unusual urgency. The outward display of religion must not entice the passionate and hungry, turning them away from the truth of the gospel. Paul's heart burns as he looks to the end of his journey and knows that death is near. He stirs our conscience with his emotional letter.

The urgency of this letter is Paul's revelation of the last days. Mentioned here in 2 Timothy more than any other letter, Paul warns, instructs, and challenges all of us to live a life of purity as the days grow evil. He gives us six analogies of the last days' servant of the Lord. The believer is compared to a soldier (2:3), an athlete (2:5), a farmer (2:6), a minister (2:15), a container (2:21), and a servant (2:24).

I believe there are many verses that could be considered the most important themes of the book, but perhaps 4:7–8 would contain the summary theme of the letter:

> I have fought an excellent fight. I have finished
> my full course and I've kept my heart full of faith.
> There's a crown of righteousness waiting in heaven
> for me, and I know that my Lord will reward me on
> his day of righteous judgment. And this crown is not
> only waiting for me, but for all who love and long
> for his unveiling.

As you read 2 Timothy, try to picture Paul sitting in a prison cell. He misses his wonderful disciple Timothy. Picture Timothy reading this letter with a longing deep within to hear these final words from his spiritual dad. Their love is deep, their commitment to the gospel is powerful, and their desire to see the world reached with the love of Christ is real.

PURPOSE

Writing from prison and awaiting execution, Paul seeks to impart his final words of wisdom to his spiritual son Timothy. He carries some of the concerns over from his first letter, such as dealing with false teachers. In this letter, however, Paul weaves together the themes of suffering, perseverance, and vindication in relation to his own experience and Christ's. Paul gives Timothy this example to encourage him in his own ministry, and also his Christian life.

AUTHOR AND AUDIENCE

Written in AD 65 shortly before his martyrdom at the order of the Roman Emperor Nero, Paul wants to make sure Timothy is instructed about serving the church as God's man. There is a spiritual inheritance found in 2 Timothy for every true minister of the gospel and for every lover of God.

Many have recognized this letter as the most personal and heartfelt of all of Paul's writings. He names twenty-three individuals—both friends and foes. He opens his heart and gives intimate details of his life, and he shares his desire to see Timothy advance in his calling.

Apparently, Timothy is still in Ephesus fulfilling the mandate Paul gave him in his first letter. Paul writes to his spiritual son knowing that death is near. He longed to see Timothy again and desired to make sure he was encouraged to finish his race to the end.

MAJOR THEMES

False Teachers and Doctrine. Apparently the same situation of unorthodox teaching Paul addressed in his first letter was still a problem. This time Paul calls these false teachers out by name: Hymenaeus and Philetus "are like gangrene," he says, who "have already spread their poison to many" (2:17). He urges Timothy to unapologetically preach the Word of Truth and stay away from their foolish arguments.

Suffering and Perseverance. From a Roman prison, waiting to be executed, Paul urges his gospel coworker to suffer as he has for the gospel. Paul calls Timothy into such living not only because of his own willingness to suffer but also because of Christ's own experience of death. He drives home this calling for courage by offering shameful examples of believers who've betrayed such a calling. Instead, Timothy—and we—are called to persevere through suffering like Paul, and like Christ, in order to receive their reward.

Faithfulness in Life and Ministry. As you might expect from a last will and testament, Paul instructs Timothy to pick up where he left off by carrying out his ministry with dedication and faithfully preaching the apostolic message. Paul offers his own life as an example of the kind of faithfulness to ministry and godliness he is urging Timothy to follow.

2 TIMOTHY

Heaven's Urgency

Introduction

1 From Paul, an apostle of Jesus the Messiah, appointed by God's pleasure to announce the wonderful promise of life found in Jesus, the anointed Messiah.

²My beloved son, I pray for a greater release of God's grace, love, and total well-being to flow into your life from God our Father and from our Lord Jesus Christ!

³You know that I've been called to serve the God of my fathers with a clean conscience. Night and day I pray constantly for you, building a memorial for you with my prayers. ⁴I know that you have wept for me, your spiritual father, and your tears are dear to me. I can't wait to see you again! I'm filled with joy ⁵as I think of your strong faith *that was passed down through your family line.* It began with your grandmother Lois, who passed it on to your dear mother, Eunice. And it's clear that you too are following in the footsteps of their godly example.

Timothy and the Holy Spirit

⁶I'm writing to encourage you to fan into a flame and rekindle*ᵃ* the fire of the spiritual gift God imparted to you when I laid my hands *upon you.* ⁷For God will never give you the spirit of fear,*ᵇ* but the Holy Spirit who gives

---

a 1:6 Literally "excite the gift" or "awake the gift."

b 1:7 That is, fearing men. The fear of God prevents us from fearing others.

you mighty power, love, and self-control.[a] [8]So never be ashamed of the testimony of our Lord, nor be embarrassed over my imprisonment, but overcome every evil by the revelation of the power of God![b] [9]He gave us resurrection life[c] and drew us to himself by his holy calling on our lives. And it wasn't because of any good we have done, but by his divine pleasure and marvelous grace that confirmed our union with the anointed Jesus, even before time began![d] [10]This truth is now being unveiled by the revelation of the anointed Jesus, our life-giver, who has dismantled death, *obliterating all its effects on our lives*, and has manifested his immortal life in us by the gospel.

Paul and His Gospel Ministry

[11]And he has anointed[e] me as his preacher, his apostle, and his teacher of truth to the nations. [12]The confidence of my calling enables me to overcome every difficulty without shame, for I have an intimate revelation of this God. And my faith in him convinces me that he is more than able to keep all that I've placed in his hands[f] safe and secure until the fullness of his appearing.

[13]Allow the healing words you've heard from me to live in you and make them a model for life as your faith and love for the Anointed One *grows even more*. [14]Guard well this incomparable treasure by the Spirit of Holiness living within you.

---

a 1:7 The Aramaic can also be translated "revelation-light," or "instruction."

b 1:8 Or "with the gospel and the power of God."

c 1:9 Or "He is our life-giver."

d 1:9 Literally "before the time of the ages."

e 1:11 Or "consecrated."

f 1:12 Or "what he has entrusted to me."

¹⁵Perhaps you've heard that Phygelus,^a and Hermogenes^b and all the believers of Asia have deserted me because of my imprisonment. ¹⁶Nevertheless, so many times Onesiphorus^c was like a breath of fresh air to me and never seemed to be ashamed of my chains. May our Lord Jesus bestow compassion and mercy upon him and his household. ¹⁷For when he arrived in Rome, he searched and searched for me until he found out *where I was being held, so that he could minister to me,* ¹⁸just like he did so wonderfully as I rested in his house^d while in Ephesus, as you well know.

May Jesus, our Master, give him abundant mercy in the day he stands before him.

Grace to Overcome

2 Timothy, my dear son,^e live your life empowered by God's free-flowing grace, which is your true strength, found in the anointing of Jesus *and your union with him*! ²And all that you've learned from me, confirmed by the integrity of my life,^f deposit into faithful leaders who are competent to teach the congregations the same revelation.

---

a 1:15 His name means "fugitive."

b 1:15 His name means "born of Hermes," a pagan god.

c 1:16 His name means "one who brings profit" or "profitable" or "help-bringer." The Orthodox tradition recognizes Onesiphorus as one of the seventy disciples chosen and sent by Jesus to preach. He became a bishop at Colophon (Asia Minor) and later at Corinth. Both the Orthodox and Roman Catholic churches hold that he died a martyr outside of Ephesus in the city of Parium.

d 1:18 This is an alternate translation of the Aramaic words found in v. 16. This translation has placed them here for the sake of the English narrative.

e 2:1 The Greek text literally means "my little child," and is used as a term of endearment.

f 2:2 Or "by way of many witnesses." These "witnesses" could be those people who also heard Paul's teaching, or it may refer to the prophetic confirmations of the truth he taught to Timothy.

[3]Overcome every form of evil[a] as a victorious soldier of Jesus the Anointed One. [4]For every soldier called to active duty must divorce himself from the distractions of this world so that he may fully satisfy the one who chose him.

[5]An athlete who doesn't play by the rules will never receive the trophy, *so remain faithful to God!*[b]

[6]The farmer who labors to produce a crop should be the first one to be fed from its harvest.

[7]Carefully consider all that I've taught you, and may our Lord inspire you with wisdom and revelation *in everything you say and do.* [8]But make Jesus, the Anointed One, your focus in life and ministry. For he came to earth as the descendant of David and rose from the dead, according to the revelation of the gospel that God has given me. [9]This is the reason I am persecuted and imprisoned *by evildoers,*[c] enduring the suffering of these chains—but the Word of God can never be chained! [10]I endure all these hardships for the benefit of the chosen ones[d] in Christ so that they may also discover the overcoming life that is in Jesus Christ, and experience a glory that lasts forever!

[11]You can trust these words:

If we were joined with him in his death, then we are joined with him in his life! [12]If we are joined with

---

a 2:3 As translated from the Aramaic. The Greek says "suffer hardships."

b 2:5 Supplied by the context to complete the ellipsis.

c 2:9 The Greek text means "imprisoned as a criminal." However, the Aramaic word used here for "persecuted" can also be translated "crucified." Perhaps Paul is giving a prophecy of what would come. Later, Paul was indeed martyred either by crucifixion or beheading for his faith in Christ.

d 2:10 The Greek word here for "chosen" has embedded within it the word *logos.* God's chosen ones have been chosen by the word of God to become a living word sent from his mouth to reveal the message of their destiny.

him in his sufferings,ᵃ then we will reign together
with him in his triumph. But if we disregard him,
then he will also disregard us. ¹³But even if we are
faithless, he will still be full of faith, for he never
wavers in his faithfulness to us!ᵇ

¹⁴Be committed to teach the believers all these things
when you are with them in the presence of the Lord. Instruct
them to never be drawn into meaningless arguments, or
tear each other down with useless words that only harm
others.

¹⁵Always be eagerᶜ to present yourself before God as a
perfect and mature minister, without shame, as one who
correctly explains the Word of Truth.

Avoid False Teachings

¹⁶And avoid empty chatter and worthless words,ᵈ for they
simply add to the irreverence of those who converse in
that manner. ¹⁷For the words of Hymenaeusᵉ and Philetus
are like gangrene, *they have already spread their poison
to many.* ¹⁸They are lost to the truth *and teach gross error
when* they teach that the resurrection of the dead has

ᵃ 2:12 An alternate Aramaic translation could read "If we preach the
kingdom, we shall rule with him."

ᵇ 2:13 Or "he will not be unfaithful to himself."

ᶜ 2:15 An alternate Aramaic translation is "Don't become frustrated."
The Greek word is *spoudazo*, an aorist imperative verb that could
be translated, "Hurry and keep on hurrying," or "Consider it a serious matter and keep on considering it something serious to present
yourself before God."

ᵈ 2:16 The Greek text could be translated "avoid corrupt and useless
speakers," referring not to the words themselves, but to those who
teach the flock. See v. 18.

ᵉ 2:17 See the first footnote for 1 Tim. 1:20.

already passed.[a] They are guilty of subverting[b] the faith of some believers.

[19]But the firm[c] foundation of God has written upon it these two inscriptions: "The Lord God recognizes those who are truly his!"[d] and, "Everyone who worships the name of the Lord Jesus[e] must forsake wickedness!"[f]

Be a Pure Container of Christ

[20]In a palace you find many kinds of containers and table-ware for many different uses. Some are beautifully inlaid with gold or silver, but some are made of wood or earthenware; some of them are used for banquets and special occasions, and some for everyday use. [21]But you, Timothy, must not see your life and ministry this way. *Your life and ministry must not be disgraced*, for you are to be a pure container of Christ and dedicated to the honorable purposes of your Master, prepared[g] for every good work that he gives you to do.

[22]Run as fast as you can from all the ambitions and lusts[h] of youth; and chase after all that is pure. Whatever builds up your faith and deepens your love must become your holy pursuit. And live in peace with all those who worship our Lord Jesus with pure hearts.

[23]Stay away from all the foolish arguments of the imma-ture, for these disputes will only generate more conflict.

---

a 2:18 The Aramaic can be translated "never going to happen."

b 2:18 The Greek literally means "turning upside down the faith of some."

c 2:19 Or "true." An alternate Aramaic translation of this verse could read "that resurrection is the firm foundation," referring to v. 18.

d 2:19 See Num. 16:5.

e 2:19 Or "Lord." By implication it is the Lord Jesus.

f 2:19 An alternate Aramaic translation could read "He will save from wickedness."

g 2:21 The Aramaic can be translated "appreciated."

h 2:22 The Greek text literally means "revolutionary desires."

²⁴For a true servant of our Lord Jesus will not be argumentative[a] but gentle toward all and skilled in helping others see the truth, having great patience toward the immature. ²⁵Then with meekness you'll be able to carefully enlighten those who argue with you so they can see God's gracious gift of repentance and be brought to the truth. ²⁶This will cause them to rediscover themselves[b] and escape from the snare of Satan who caught them in his trap so that they would carry out his purposes.

Characteristics of the Last Days

3 But you need to be aware that in the final days the culture of society will become extremely fierce. ²People will be self-centered lovers of themselves[c] and obsessed with money. They will boast of great things as they strut around in their arrogant pride and mock all that is right. They will ignore their own families.[d] They will be ungrateful[e] and ungodly.

³They will become addicted to hateful and malicious slander.[f] Slaves to their desires, they will be ferocious, belligerent haters of what is good and right. ⁴With brutal treachery, they will act without restraint, bigoted and wrapped in clouds of their conceit. They will find their delight in the pleasures of this world more than the pleasures of the loving God.

---

a 2:24 An alternate Aramaic translation could read "You should not be argumentative with a true servant of the Lord."

b 2:26 Or "come to their senses."

c 3:2 The Aramaic can be translated "men will look out only for themselves."

d 3:2 Or "disloyal to their people." The Greek is "disobedient to parents."

e 3:2 The Aramaic can be translated "rejecters of grace."

f 3:3 Because this phrase is also the description of the devil (the accuser or slanderer), it could be translated "they will be devils."

⁵They may pretend to have a respect for God, but in reality they want nothing to do with God's power. Stay away from people like these! ⁶For they are the ones who worm their way into the hearts of vulnerable women,ᵃ spending the night with those who are captured by their lusts and steeped in sin. ⁷They are always learning but never discover the revelation-knowledge of truth.

⁸*History has given us an example of this with the Egyptian sorcerers* Jannes and Jambres,ᵇ who stood against Moses in their arrogance. So it will be in the last days with those who reject the faith with their corrupt minds and arrogant hearts, standing against the truth of God.

⁹But they will not advance, for everyone will see their madness, just as they did with *Jannes and Jambres!*ᶜ

Timothy's Loyalty

¹⁰But you, Timothy, have closely followed my example and the truth that I've imparted to you. You have modeled your life after the love and endurance *I've demonstrated in my ministry by not giving up.* The faith I have, *you now have.* What I have hungered for in life has now become *your longing as well.* The patience I have with others, *you now demonstrate.* ¹¹And the same persecutions and difficulties I have endured, *you have also endured.* Yes,

---

a 3:6 An alternate Greek translation could read "they intrude into households and by their heresies, take prisoners of those who are led astray by desires and sins." The Aramaic, however, is clearly speaking of the gross immorality of the last days.

b 3:8 This is a fascinating verse, for Jannes and Jambres are never mentioned by name in Exodus. It simply mentions the sorcerers who wanted to compete with Moses and his authority. These two names are, however, mentioned by Origen, one of the church fathers, who makes reference to the Book of Jannes and Jambres, but no complete copies of these books have ever been found.

c 3:9 Implied in the conclusion of Paul's argument.

you know all about what I had to suffer while in Antioch, Iconium, and Lystra. You're aware of all the persecution I endured there; yet the Lord delivered me from every single one of them! [12]For all who choose to live godly as worshipers of Jesus, the Anointed One, will also experience persecution.

[13]But the evil men and sorcerers[a] will progress from bad to worse, deceived and deceiving, as they lead people further from the truth. [14]Yet you must continue to advance in strength with the truth wrapped around your heart, being assured by God that he's the One[b] who has truly taught you all these things.

[15]Remember what you were taught from your childhood from the Holy Scrolls[c] which can impart to you wisdom to experience everlasting life through the faith of Jesus, the Anointed One! [16]God has transmitted his very substance into every Scripture,[d] for it is God-breathed.[e] It will empower you by its instruction and correction, giving you the strength to take the right direction and lead you deeper into the path of godliness. [17]Then you will be God's servant, fully mature and perfectly prepared to fulfill any assignment God gives you.

---

a 3:13 Or "deceivers." The Greek word is "sorcerers."

b 3:14 By implication "God." However, some interpret this as his teachers.

c 3:15 Or "sacred Scriptures."

d 3:16 Keep in mind that when Paul wrote this he was referring to the Torah and all the Old Testament writings. Today, "every Scripture" would include the New Testament as well.

e 3:16 The Word of God is inspired. Scripture is not simply a book that tells about God, it actually contains God. His breath is embedded in his Word.

Paul's Farewell Message

4 Timothy, in the presence[a] of our great God and our Lord Jesus Christ, the One who is destined to judge both the living and the dead by the revelation of his kingdom—I solemnly instruct you to [2]proclaim the Word of God *and stand upon it no matter what*! Rise to the occasion and preach when it is convenient and when it is not. Preach in the full expression of the Holy Spirit[b]—with wisdom and patience as you instruct and teach the people.

[3]For the time is coming when they will no longer listen and respond to the healing words of truth *because they will become selfish and proud*. They will seek out teachers with soothing words that line up with their desires, saying just what they want to hear. [4]They will close their ears to the truth and believe nothing but fables and myths.[c] [5]So be alert to all these things and overcome every form of evil. Carry in your heart the passion of your calling as *a church planter[d]* and evangelist, and fulfill your ministry calling.[e]

[6]And now the time is fast approaching for my release from this life and I am ready to be offered as a sacrifice.[f] [7]I have fought an excellent fight. I have finished my full course *with all my might* and I've kept my heart full of faith. [8]There's a crown of righteousness waiting in

---

a 4:1 Or "before the eyes of God." The Greek word is *enopion*, which could be translated "within eyesight of." Imagine looking into heaven and seeing the eyes of God gazing at you. This is the strength of Paul's charge to Timothy.

b 4:2 As translated from the Aramaic.

c 4:4 The Aramaic can be translated "ritualistic ceremonies."

d 4:5 Implied in the concept of being a New Testament evangelist. Apostolic missionaries sent out to evangelize were to plant churches wherever they ministered. Our contemporary concept of an evangelist is quite different than in Paul's day.

e 4:5 Or "being confident in your ministry."

f 4:6 Or "poured out as a drink offering."

heaven for me, and I know that my Lord will reward me on his day of righteous judgment. And this crown is not only waiting for me, but for all who love and long for his unveiling.[a]

[9]Please come as soon as you can [10]since Demas deserted me and has left to go to Thessalonica, for he loves his own life.[b] Crescens has gone to Galatia, and Titus has gone to Dalmatia. [11]That leaves only Luke with me, so find Mark and bring him with you, for he is a tremendous help for me in my ministry.

[12]I have also dispatched Tychicus to Ephesus to minister there. [13]When you come, please bring the leather book bag[c] along with the books I left in Troas with Carpus—especially the parchment scrolls.

[14]You need to know that Alexander,[d] the jeweler,[e] has done me great harm. May our Lord give him what he deserves for all he has done. [15]Be careful of him, for he arrogantly opposes our ministry.

[16]At first there was no one I could count on to faithfully stand with me—they all ran off and abandoned me—but don't hold this against them. [17]*For in spite of this*, my Lord himself stood with me, empowering me to complete my

---

a 4:8 Or "sudden appearance."

b 4:10 Or "he loves the world."

c 4:13 The Aramaic can be translated "carrying case." This would have been a bag made of leather or woolen cloth. The Greek text reads "bring the cloak." The Aramaic words for "book" and "cloak" are nearly identical, which would explain the Greek mistranslation using "cloak." It is fascinating that the aged Paul, nearing death, found his heart attached to the manuscripts and books that undoubtedly expounded on the Old Testament writings. He knew Jesus intimately, yet longed for more revelation of the written Word until his death.

d 4:14 *Alexander* means "protector of men" or "man-pleaser."

e 4:14 The word used here can also be "silversmith," "blacksmith" or "coppersmith."

ministry of preaching to all the non-Jewish nations so they all could hear the message and be delivered from the mouth of the lion![a] [18]And my Lord will continue to deliver me from every form of evil and give me life in his heavenly kingdom. May all the glory go to him alone for all the ages of eternity!

[19]Please give my warm regards[b] to Prisca and to Aquila[c] and to Onesiphorus and his family.

[20]Erastus has remained in Corinth, but Trophimus I had to leave in Miletus due to his illness.[d]

[21]Do your best to come before winter.

Eubulus sends his greetings, along with Pudens, Linus,[e] and Claudia, and all those in prison with me.

[22]The Lord is within your spirit and his grace overflows to you!

Love in Christ,
Paul

---

a 4:17 Or "that they will hear that I have been delivered from the mouth of the lion." By implication, the lion is a metaphor for the devil.

b 4:19 The Aramaic can be translated "give peace."

c 4:19 *Prisca* is a diminutive form of Priscilla ("long life"). She and her husband, Aquila ("eagle"), were tentmakers like Paul. They were not only business partners with Paul, but also partners with him in ministry. See Acts 18:2, 18, 26; Rom. 16:3; 1 Cor. 16:19.

d 4:20 The Greek word used here can refer to physical or spiritual ailments.

e 4:21 In church history it was widely accepted and stated by Irenaeus that Linus was a disciple of Peter and became the bishop of Rome.

TITUS

Introduction

AT A GLANCE

Author: The apostle Paul
Audience: Titus, Paul's "true son"
Date: AD 57, possibly 62–63
Type of Literature: A letter
Major Themes: Salvation, church leadership, and right living
Outline:
Letter Opening — 1:1–4
Instructions to Titus — 1:5–16
Instructions for Godly Living — 2:1–3:11
Letter Closing — 3:12–15

ABOUT TITUS

Who was this friend of Paul named Titus? He was a Greek convert from Antioch and an apostolic church planter, much like Timothy, his peer. Paul describes him as a "true son" (1:4). He was likely a convert of Paul's ministry during his visit to Cyprus. Legend has it that Titus was a poet and a student of Greek philosophy when he had a prophetic dream that led him to study the Word of God and to become a Christ-follower. As God's faithful servant he traveled with Paul on his third missionary journey (2 Cor. 2:12–13; 7:5–15; 8:6–24). Paul commends him for his love, for his steadfast faith, and for bringing comfort to God's people.

After leaving Timothy in Ephesus, Paul accompanied Titus to Crete and left him there to establish the young church and set things in order. Believers who had been in the upper room had returned to Crete (Acts 2:11) and were in need of guidance and leadership from Titus.

Some say Paul wrote his letter to Titus as early as AD 57 from Nicopolis, prior to writing 2 Timothy. Others assume that he wrote this letter around the same time as he wrote his first letter to another young leader, Timothy, around 62–63.

Titus is one of three letters commonly known as the Pastoral Epistles, which also include 1 and 2 Timothy. Paul wrote them as an older apostle to his younger colleagues, Timothy and Titus, to encourage their ministries among God's people and to give further instructions to the churches he had planted.

The theme of Titus is that right living will always accompany right doctrine. Good words will flow from a solid understanding of God's Word. In today's culture, it is easy to say that we follow Christ, but our faith in him will be demonstrated by godly living. An understanding of truth will bring a demonstration of purity through our lives. God's saving grace is the same grace that empowers us to live for him.

The book of Titus reminds us that right beliefs should impact every area of our lives: family, relationships, work, and community.

PURPOSE

Like his letters to Timothy, Paul wrote this letter to Titus in order to give him instructions for building churches and raising up leaders. It was to be considered as a church-planting manual, helping this young apostle to encourage godly living and to establish godly churches.

It appears that Paul's first letter to Timothy and this one to Titus were both written around the same time, given the close parallels in the themes addressed. From church administration to confronting false teaching to maintaining the purity of personal conduct, Paul offered sage advice and pastoral wisdom to these young ministers. In the case of Titus, Paul wrote to address basic catechesis relevant to new believers, as well as the kinds of problems expected of a young church in a pagan culture. He also wrote his former companion to ask him to remain in Crete and care for the young church in Paul's absence, as well as to encourage the two companions accompanying the letter.

AUTHOR AND AUDIENCE

As with the two letters to Timothy, Paul's letter to Titus is a deeply personal one, for it was written from mentor to mentee—from an older, wiser, seasoned apostle to a younger, inexperienced minister. It's a letter between former colleagues on the frontline of missions, as Paul sought to give roots to the work they had started together by nurturing the community of believers through Titus's leadership.

Like Timothy, Paul had left Titus among his own ethnic people to continue the work they had started as a team; in this case, on the Greek island of Crete. As a convert of Paul, his "true son in the faith" (1:4), Titus became a trusted colleague in his gospel work. In fact, many believe the two made a missionary journey to Crete to evangelize the Greek island, occurring after the events of Acts 28 and before writing 2 Timothy, when Paul was imprisoned. As a young pastor stewarding a young church plant, Titus must have viewed Paul's letter as a welcomed breeze inflating the sails of his ministry!

MAJOR THEMES

Faith and Salvation in Jesus Christ. You would expect a letter from one ministry colleague to another to center on the good news of salvation in Christ. And Titus is indeed infused with it! After laboring alongside each other to proclaim the gospel, Paul recognized that their work was unfinished. He wanted Titus "to further the faith of God's chosen ones and lead them to the full knowledge of the truth that leads to godliness" (1:1) by discipling the young church in their shared salvation.

Part of how Paul emphasized this faith and salvation was by calling on Titus to appoint godly leaders to serve as examples to teach the faith, lead people to salvation, refute false teachings that destroy faith and distract from this salvation, and imitate the practical results of this faith: godly living resulting from salvation.

He also offered a basic catechism, or summary of primary Christian beliefs. He reminded them of the grace manifested in Jesus and the salvation he brought for all. He also reminded them of their previous fallen nature, how they "were easily led astray as slaves to worldly passions and pleasures" and "wasted [their] lives in doing evil" (3:3). And he shared with them a royal "hymn of salvation by grace," which declared the wonders of God's compassion, his overflowing love, and our new birth through our salvation by faith.

Appointing Church Leadership. The work of salvation among God's people and sharing the gospel within culture requires leaders who are of sound character and judgment. As he did with Timothy, Paul instructed Titus to appoint church leaders (elders or overseers) who were blameless, faithful in marriage and had well-behaved children, gentle and patient, and never drunk, violent, or greedy. They were to set an example for the rest of the community of believers in how they should live the truth of the gospel through godly living. They were also to firmly grasp the gospel message taught to them, in order to teach other believers the essential truths of the faith and how to respond to false teaching. This rubric for spirit-anointed leaders still serves as a trusted guide for church leadership.

Right Living for the Sake of the Gospel. Right living (orthopraxy) and right believing (orthodoxy) go hand in hand in Paul's letter to Titus. For when we believe in the gospel, and experience the joys of salvation, how else could we live other than in light of this mercy?

One thing Paul emphasizes, however, is that the gospel's grace actually trains us to live rightly. "This same grace," says Paul, "teaches us how to live each day as we turn our backs on ungodliness and indulgent lifestyles, and it equips us to live self-controlled, upright, godly lives in this present age" (2:12). Paul also emphasizes the need for godly men and women within the church to come alongside others to teach them to live rightly. May our right believing never excuse wrong living. And may our right living be evidence of our right believing.

TITUS

A Godly Life

Introduction

1 From Paul, God's willing slave[a] and an apostle of Jesus, the Anointed One, *to Titus.*[b] I'm writing to you to further the faith[c] of God's chosen ones and lead them to the full knowledge of the truth that leads to godliness, [2]which rests on the hope of eternal life. God, who never lies,[d] has promised this before time began. [3]In his own time he unveiled his word through the preaching *of the gospel*, which was entrusted to me by the command of God our Life Giver.[e]

[4]Titus, you are my true son in the faith we share. May grace and peace descend to you from God the Father and our Savior, the Anointed One, Jesus!

---

a 1:1 Or "bondservant."

b 1:1 Although the name Titus is not found until v. 4, it is included here to enhance the understanding of Paul's introduction.

c 1:1 Or "according to the faith of God's elect."

d 1:2 Paul is making quite a statement in this verse. Zeus was said to have been born in Crete, and Cretans were known to be liars (1:12). So Paul is saying to the Cretans that our God is greater than Zeus and he never lies!

e 1:3 As translated from the Aramaic. The Greek is "Savior."

Qualities of Church Leaders

[5]The reason I stationed you in Crete[a] was so that you could set things in order and complete what was left unfinished,[b] and *to raise up and* appoint *church* elders[c] in every city, just as I had instructed you. [6]Each of them must be above reproach, devoted solely to his wife,[d] whose children are believers and not rebellious or out of control. [7]The overseer, since he serves God's household,[e] must be someone of blameless character and not be opinionated or short-tempered. He must not be a drunkard or violent or greedy. [8]Instead he should be one who is known for his hospitality and a lover of goodness.[f] He should be recognized as one who is fair-minded, pure-hearted, and self-controlled. [9]He must have a firm grasp of the trustworthy message that he has been taught. This will enable him to both encourage others with healthy teachings and provide convincing answers to those who oppose his message.

---

a 1:5 A Greek island in the Aegean Sea. Paul's ship had stopped on the way to Rome at Fair Havens, a small harbor on the southern coast of Crete (Acts 27:7–12).

b 1:5 The unfinished work would be bringing believers into maturity in Christ and raising up godly, qualified leaders who could teach the church and lead it forward.

c 1:5 Or "ordain elders." This is the Greek word *presbyteros*, which means "senior leaders." These are church elders who would function as overseers, teachers, and shepherds of God's flock. The same Greek word is used for women in 1 Tim. 5:2. Although generally assumed to be male in the cultural context of that day, there is nothing to indicate that *presbyteros* is gender exclusive. The church elder is called an "overseer" (or "bishop") in v. 7, which indicates that both terms speak of the same office and are synonymous.

d 1:6 Or "the husband of one wife" or "married only once."

e 1:7 Or "God's steward."

f 1:8 The Aramaic can be translated "one who nurtures goodness" (in others). We would say, "one who brings out the best in others."

False Teachers

¹⁰There are many wayward people, smooth talkers, and deceivers—especially the converts from Judaism.ᵃ ¹¹They must be silencedᵇ because they are disrupting entire families with their corrupt teachings, all for their dishonest greed. ¹²A certain one of them, one of their own prophets,ᶜ said, "Those Cretans are nothing but liars, worthless beasts, and lazy gluttons."ᵈ ¹³He certainly knew what he was talking about! For this reason, correct them thoroughly so that their lives will line up with the truths of our faith. ¹⁴Instruct them not to pay any attention to Jewish myths or follow the teachings of those who reject the truth.

¹⁵*It's true that* all is pure to those who have pure hearts, but to the corrupt unbelievers nothing is pure. Their minds and consciences are defiled. ¹⁶They claim to know God, but by their actions they deny him. They are disgusting, disobedient, and disqualified from doing anything good.

Character Consistent with Godliness

2 Your duty is to teach them to embrace a lifestyle that is consistent with sound doctrine. ²Lead the male eldersᵉ into disciplined lives full of dignity and self-control. Urge

---

ᵃ 1:10 Or "those of the circumcision" (group), i.e., Jewish converts. Paul is pointing to three types of people who will refute and argue with church leaders: rebels, empty talkers, and deceivers. The leaders (elders) must be faithful to the Scriptures in order to correct them and set them in order.

ᵇ 1:11 Or "reined in." The Greek word *epistomizo* is used for the reins of a horse.

ᶜ 1:12 Although the Greek uses the word *prophet*, it is not used here in the biblical sense of a "prophet" of God, for the author of this proverb was a pagan.

ᵈ 1:12 A quote from the Oracles of Epimenides, a six-century BC poet. The first line is quoted from The *Hymn to Zeus* by Callimachus.

ᵉ 2:2 Or "old men."

them to have a solid faith, generous love, and patient endurance.

³Likewise with the female elders,ᵃ lead them into lives free from gossip and drunkenness and to be teachers of beautiful things.ᵇ ⁴This will enable them to teach the younger womenᶜ to love their husbands, to love their children, ⁵and to be self-controlled and pure, taking care of their household and being devoted toᵈ their husbands. By doing these things the word of God will not be discredited.

⁶Likewise, guide the younger men into living disciplined lives *for Christ.*

Be an Example
⁷Above all, set yourself apart as a model of a life nobly lived. With dignity, demonstrate integrity in all that you teach.ᵉ ⁸Bring a clear, wholesome messageᶠ that cannot be condemned, and then your critics will be embarrassed, with nothing bad to say about us.ᵍ

⁹Servantsʰ are to be supportive ofⁱ their masters and do what is pleasing in every way. They are not to be

---

a 2:3 Or "old women."
b 2:3 As translated from the Aramaic. The Greek is "good things."
c 2:4 Paul is contrasting the "elders" with the "younger" (Gr. *neos*) and could possibly be referring to those who are newly converted.
d 2:5 Or "supportive of."
e 2:7 "Integrity in all that you teach" would imply serious study of God's Word and its personal application in our lives, and not teaching impulsively from one's opinion, which only leads to arguments and divisions. This kind of integrity gives someone the right to be heard.
f 2:8 Or "with sound speech."
g 2:8 Paul and Titus were a team. If one were to err, it would affect the other.
h 2:9 Or "bondservants."
i 2:9 Or "submitted to."

argumentative [10]nor steal[a] but prove themselves to be completely loyal and trustworthy. By doing this they will advertise[b] through all that they do the beautiful teachings of God our Savior.

God's Grace, Our Motivation

[11]God's marvelous grace[c] has manifested *in person*, bringing salvation for everyone.[d] [12]This same grace teaches us how to live each day as we turn our backs on ungodliness and indulgent lifestyles,[e] and it equips us to live self-controlled, upright, godly lives in this present age.[f] [13]For we continue to wait for the fulfillment of our hope in the dawning splendor[g] of the glory of our great God and

---

a 2:10 Businesses today lose millions of dollars to employee theft. Believers are to be meticulously honest in the workplace.

b 2:10 Or "adorn [beautify] the doctrine of God."

c 2:11 Grace extends God's kindness and love to us every moment and makes us "worthy" of his acceptance. Grace is unconditional, unmerited, indescribable favor from God.

d 2:11 That is, grace has revealed a salvation available for everyone. Or "God's marvelous grace has appeared to all, bringing salvation."

e 2:12 The Greek word for "ungodliness" is singular, while the word for "indulgent lifestyles" is plural. This has led some scholars to believe that we are to turn our backs on both the root principle of ungodliness and the specific acts that result from ungodliness.

f 2:12 These three adjectives—"self-controlled," "upright," and "godly"—refer to our behavior, our behavior toward others and toward God.

g 2:13 Or "the blessed hope and glorious appearing." The Greek word is *epiphaneia* (epiphany) and is a nominalized verb that means "a brightness shining all around." It was through *epiphaneia*, the beautiful appearing of Christ as a baby, that a wonderful hope was brought to all the world.

Savior, Jesus, the Anointed One.[a] [14]He sacrificed himself for us that he might purchase our freedom from every lawless deed and to purify for himself a people who are his very own,[b] passionate to do what is beautiful in his eyes.

[15]So preach these truths and exhort others to follow them. Be willing to expose sin in order to bring correction with full authority,[c] without being intimidated[d] by anyone.

Believers' Conduct in Society

3 Remind people to respect[e] their governmental leaders on every level as law-abiding citizens and to be ready to fulfill their civic duty. [2]*And remind them* to never tear down anyone with their words or quarrel,[f] but instead be considerate, humble, and courteous to everyone. [3]For it

---

a 2:13 Or "our great God and our Savior, Jesus Christ." Note the four great truths of grace in vv. 11–13: (1) Grace is a person—"our great God and Savior, Jesus, the Anointed One." (2) Grace brings salvation for all. (3) Grace educates us on how to live pure lives. (4) Grace brings a hope of the manifestation (appearing) of Christ. This is a hope worth waiting for.

b 2:14 We are a people encircled by God himself. The compound Greek word *periousios* is translated from "around," as a circle, and the verb "to be." It can mean something surrounded by something. It can be charted by a dot within a circle. As the circle surrounds the dot, so God is around each one of his saints. The circle has the dot all to itself. So God has his very own all to himself. We are unique in that we belong only to him. Uniquely his, we are monopolized by God, taken into himself by grace through faith and surrounded by his love.

c 2:15 Or "Speak these things; exhort or rebuke [speak in order to expose sin and bring correction] with all authority."

d 2:15 Or "disregarded."

e 3:1 Or "be subject to."

f 3:2 Or "strive with others." The implication is that we accept the differences of others and allow people to be who they are and not try to make them over into our image of who we think they should be.

wasn't that long ago that we behaved foolishly in our stubborn disobedience. We were easily led astray as slaves to worldly passions and pleasures. We wasted our lives in doing evil, and with hateful jealousy we hated others.

The Hymn of Salvation by Grace

⁴When the extraordinary compassion of God our
Savior*a*
and his overpowering love suddenly appeared *in
person,*
as the brightness of a dawning day,ᵇ
⁵he came to save us.
Not because of any virtuous deed that we have done
but only because of his extravagant mercy.
⁶He saved us,
resurrecting us*c* through the washing of rebirth.
We are made completely new by the Holy Spirit,*d*
whom he splashed over us
richly
by Jesus, the Messiah, our Life Giver.
⁷So as a gift of his love,
and since we are faultless—
innocent before his face—
we can now become heirs *of all things,*
all because of an overflowing hope of eternal life.

⁸How true and faithful is this message!

---

a 3:4 Many scholars believe that vv. 4–7 are ancient Christian poetry or perhaps the words to a hymn.

b 3:4 Implied in the Greek word *epiphainō* (epiphany), which means "to shine forth [brightly] in an appearing."

c 3:6 As translated from the Aramaic.

d 3:6 All three members of the Trinity are mentioned in vv. 4–6 and are seen as active participants in our salvation.

Faith Produces Good Works

I want you to especially emphasize[a] these truths, so that those who believe in God will be careful to devote themselves to doing good works. It is *always* beautiful and profitable *for believers* to do good works.

⁹But avoid useless controversies,[b] genealogies,[c] pointless quarrels, and arguments over the law, which will get you nowhere.[d] ¹⁰After a first and second warning, have nothing more to do with a divisive person *who refuses to be corrected*. ¹¹For you know that such a one is entwined with his sin and stands self-condemned.

Paul's Coworkers

¹²When I send Artemas[e] or Tychicus[f] to you, be sure to meet me at the City of Victory,[g] for I've decided to spend the winter there.

---

a 3:8 Or "affirm strongly," a hapax legomenon.

b 3:9 The Aramaic can be translated "offensive debates."

c 3:9 The Aramaic can be translated "tribal traditions."

d 3:9 See also Heb. 13:9.

e 3:12 Artemas, or "Artemas of Lystra," was considered to be one of the seventy disciples whom Jesus sent out.

f 3:12 Tychichus, an Ephesian, was a beloved coworker of Paul and is mentioned five times in the New Testament (here; Acts 20:4; Eph. 6:21; Col. 4:7; 2 Tim. 4:12). He was listed among the seventy disciples whom Jesus sent out according to Hippolytus of Rome. See Francis Mershman, "St. Tychicus" (1913) *Catholic Encyclopedia*, Charles Herbermann, editor.

g 3:12 Or "Nicopolis," a Greek city on the western shore. Nicopolis means "the City of Victory."

¹³Give a generous send-off to Zenas the scribe*a* and Apollos,*b* and send them on their journey with what they need.

Conclusion

¹⁴Encourage the believers to be passionately devoted to beautiful works of righteousness by meeting the urgent needs of others and not be unfruitful.

¹⁵Everyone here with me sends their loving greetings to you. Greet the believers who love us in the faith. May God's wonderful grace be with you all!

Love in Christ,
*Paul*c

---

a 3:13 Or "lawyer." The word translated "lawyer" can be used for either Greek or Roman law. Zenas is considered to be one of the seventy whom Jesus sent out.

b 3:13 Apollos was a powerful preacher and coworker of Paul, who was very influential in the church of Corinth. He is listed ten times in the New Testament (Acts 18:24; 19:1; 1 Cor. 1:12; 3:4–6, 22; 4:6; 16:12). Jerome states that Apollos, after Paul's letters brought healing to the divisions of the church in Corinth, returned and became an elder (overseer) in the church. See Jerome, *Commentary on the Epistle of Titus.*

c 3:15 The Aramaic adds, "The end of the letter written by Paul to Titus from Nicopolis, sent by the hand of Zenas and Apollos."

PHILEMON

Introduction

AT A GLANCE

Author: The apostle Paul
Audience: Philemon, a slave owner
Date: AD 60–61
Type of Literature: A letter
Major Themes: Christian love, Christian belonging, fellowship, and slavery
Outline:
Letter Opening — 1–3
Paul's Appreciation for Philemon — 4–7
Paul's Appeal on Behalf of Onesimus — 8–21
Letter Closing — 22–25

ABOUT PHILEMON

Paul's letter to Philemon is perhaps one of the most fascinating portions of our New Testament. It is a letter written with one purpose—to bring reconciliation between two brothers in Christ. It is a letter that promotes forgiveness as the key to unity and reconciliation. Everyone has experienced being offended, and everyone has offended another person. Yet in Christ, there is enough love to cover all sin and enough forgiveness to reconcile with those who have hurt or wounded us.

Here's the backstory of this intriguing letter: Philemon had been one of Paul's numerous coworkers in ministry. There was much history between Paul and Philemon, a person Paul considered a dear and trusted friend. It is believed that Philemon was wealthy and, along with his wife, led a dynamic house church in the city of Colossae, a city in Asia Minor (modern-day Turkey). Although Paul had never visited Colossae, there remained a strong bond of friendship between Philemon and Paul.

Apparently, Philemon owned a slave who stole from him and ran away. His name was Onesimus. (Onesimus means "useful" or "valuable." See Col. 4:9. This reference of Onesimus in Colossians suggests that Colossians was written shortly after Philemon.) By events that only God could orchestrate, the fugitive Onesimus found himself imprisoned next to Paul. Through the ministry of the Holy Spirit, Paul led his fellow prisoner to the Lord.

Paul sent the runaway slave back to Philemon carrying this letter in his hand asking his former master to fully receive Onesimus and be restored to him as a fellow believer. A slave who ran away could be punished by death according to the Roman laws of this era, yet Paul not only said Philemon should forgive him, but also love him as a brother returning home. This made-for-a-movie plot is contained in this very short letter you are about to read.

Orthodox Church tradition tells us that Onesimus served Christ faithfully throughout his life and became the bishop of the church of Ephesus after Timothy's death. The slave-turned-bishop was later taken once again as a prisoner to Rome where he testified before his judge Tertylus. He was condemned to death by stoning, and afterwards his corpse was beheaded in AD 109.

We should be grateful to God for gifting us this letter, because the dignity of every human being is brought forth powerfully in the story of Philemon and Onesimus—a story of forgiving love!

PURPOSE

The apostle Paul wrote his friend Philemon, a slave owner, mainly to encourage him to forgive and restore his slave Onesimus—and to do so no longer as a slave but as a brother in Christ. The theme of the book of Philemon is forgiving love. Love forgives, restores, covers sin, and heals broken relationships. The sweetness of reconciliation is an incomparable joy. Only the love of Christ has the power to perform such a glorious restoration of relationships. We can thank God that he has given us this amazing letter to bring hope that forgiveness is waiting—waiting for all of us to experience for ourselves.

AUTHOR AND AUDIENCE

While a prisoner for the sake of the gospel, the apostle Paul wrote to a slave owner named Philemon. Although four names are listed in the letter's opening, it was customary in ancient letters to list the primary addressee first. It is clear throughout the main body of the letter that Paul singled out a single individual in his appeal: Philemon. This letter was a precious piece of correspondence between brothers bound by Christian love.

And yet it wasn't entirely private, for two other names and "the church" were also included, revealing the important bond between brothers and sisters in their activities through their common faith in Christ. This letter becomes a window into the heart of God for Christ's community, urging generous forgiving love.

MAJOR THEMES

Christian Belonging in a Common Faith. Mentioning Apphia and Archippus, as well as Philemon's house church, turned what might have been a private conversation into a public appeal. Though Paul may have been seeking to exert some sort of social pressure on

Philemon, one of the enduring, relevant teachings of this letter is that our private business is a matter for the believing community since we belong to one another in a common faith.

Paul's use of *koinonia* (Gr. for "fellowship") in v. 6 captures this reality. When people commit themselves to Christ, they are also committing themselves to a community. They bind themselves and become identified with one another so that they receive both the benefits and responsibilities of that "belonging." Paul invited Philemon and Onesimus, in addition to the house church, to think through the radical implications of their belonging to one another as slave and master, as well as a believing community.

The Love of Christ Performed. It is clear from Paul's entire work, as well as the general tone of this letter, that his appeal was rooted in the love of Christ. Paul wanted Philemon to respond to Onesimus in forgiveness and restoration in the same way Christ has responded to us. The manner in which Paul wrote his appeal and advocated for Onesimus—his tone and tenor, his words and arguments—also reflected the tender love of Christ.

We perform the same love that Christ himself performed. Paul performed Christ's love when he advocated for Onesimus, and in the way he appealed to Philemon. And he wanted Philemon to follow his performance with his slave-turned-brother.

Slavery and Brotherhood. There's an obvious facet to the relationship between Philemon and Onesimus: slavery. To our modern ears we think of the antebellum South and the injustices of the eighteenth and nineteenth centuries. Yet slavery looked quite different in the first century, so Paul wouldn't have necessarily viewed it as sinister, and he didn't seem to offer a treatise on abolitionism in his letter.

Still Paul is clearly interested that "we no longer see each other in our former state—Jew or non-Jew, [enslaved or free] . . . because we're all one through our union with Jesus Christ with no distinction between us" (Gal. 3:28). He wanted Philemon to reflect this common union in how he treated Onesimus: "welcome him no longer as a slave, but more than that, as a dearly loved brother" (v. 16). Onesimus had gone from being a valuable slave to a valuable brother in Christ (vv. 10–11).

This letter, then, seems to be less about slavery and more about the relationship between a slave and his master, now brothers in the Lord, both of whom Paul wants to experience forgiving love.

PHILEMON

Forgiving Love

¹From Paul, a prisoner[a] of the Anointed One, Jesus, and Timothy our brother, to Philemon,[b] our precious friend and companion in this work. ²To the church that meets in his house, along with our dear sister Apphia and our fellow soldier Archippus.[c]

³May God our Father and the Lord Jesus Christ pour out his grace and peace upon you.

Philemon's Faith and Love

⁴I am always thankful to my God as I remember you in my prayers ⁵because I'm hearing reports about your faith in the Lord Jesus and how much love you have for all his holy followers. ⁶I pray for you that the faith we share[d]

---

a 1 In other letters from Paul, he describes himself as an apostle, but here, writing to his dear friend, there is no need to remind Philemon of his apostleship.

b 1 *Philemon* means "affectionate" and is derived from the Greek word *philema*, which means "kiss."

c 2 *Apphia* means "fruitful one" and is believed to be the name of Philemon's wife. *Archippus* means "master of the horse" and was possibly their son's name. See also Col. 4:17.

d 6 This is somewhat ambiguous, for the Greek is literally "for the sharing of the faith of you." It can mean a number of things, including the common faith that Paul and Philemon shared, or it could mean the faith that Philemon shared with others through evangelism. The Aramaic can be translated "May your association [fellowship] of believers [Philemon's house church] be fruitful in works and in the knowledge of all that you possess in Jesus, the Messiah."

may effectively deepen your understanding of every good thing that belongs to you in Christ. ⁷Your love *has impacted me* and brings me great joy and encouragement, for the hearts of the believers have been greatly refreshed through you, dear brother.

Paul's Request on Behalf of Onesimus

⁸Even though I have enough boldness in Christ that I could command you to do what is proper, ⁹⁻¹⁰I'd much rather make an appeal because of our friendship. So here I am, an old man,ᵃ a prisoner for Christ, making my loving appeal to you. It is on behalf of my child, whose spiritual father I becameᵇ while here in prison; that is, Onesimus.ᶜ ¹¹Formerly he was not useful or valuable to you, but now he is valuable to both of us. ¹²He is my very heart,ᵈ and I've sent him back to you *with this letter.*

¹³I would have preferred to keep him at my side so that he could take your place as my helper during my imprisonment for the sake of the gospel.ᵉ ¹⁴However, I did not want to make this decision without your consent, so that your act

---

a 9–10 Some manuscripts have "an ambassador" in place of "an old man."

b 9–10 The Aramaic can be translated "whom I birthed with my chains (while in prison)."

c 9–10 Paul employs a masterful play on words, for the name Onesimus means "useful" or "valuable." The book of Philemon is a masterpiece of grace, tact, and love.

d 12 The Aramaic can be translated "for he is my son." It would be hard to imagine a more powerful way to describe the affection between Paul and his spiritual son, Onesimus. The one who gave us the love chapter (1 Cor. 13) demonstrated that love in his relationships, even with those who were much younger than he.

e 13 Or "in the chains of the gospel." The Aramaic changes the object of the phrase to Onesimus: "I took him to serve me, chained to God's message, on your behalf."

of kindness*ª* would not be a matter of obligation but out of willingness.

¹⁵Perhaps *you could think of it this way*: he was separated from you for a short time so that you could have him back forever. ¹⁶So welcome him no longer as a slave, but more than that, as a dearly loved brother. He is that to me especially, and how much more so to you, both humanly speaking and in the Lord.

¹⁷So if you consider me your friend and partner, accept him the same way you would accept me. ¹⁸And if he has stolen anything*ᵇ* from you or owes you anything, just place it on my account.

¹⁹I, Paul, have written these words in my own handwriting. I promise to pay you back everything, to say nothing of the fact that you owe me your very self.*ᶜ*

²⁰Yes, my brother, enrich my soul*ᵈ* in the Lord—refresh my heart in Christ! ²¹I'm writing to you with confidence that you will comply with my request and do even more than what I'm asking.

²²And would you do one more thing for me? Since I'm hoping through your prayers to be restored to you soon, please prepare a guest room for me.

---

a 14 By implication, this act of kindness refers to Philemon receiving the fugitive slave back with love and forgiveness.

b 18 Although the Greek verb *adikeō* means "to do wrong" or "to defraud," the clear implication is that Onesimus had stolen from his master.

c 19 By implication, it was Paul who had brought the message of life to Philemon and became his "spiritual father" as well.

d 20 Or "benefited" or "profited." This is a play on words that would not be lost on the educated Philemon, for it is taken from the root word for "Onesimus" ("profitable").

²³Epaphras, my fellow prisoner in the Anointed One, Jesus, sends his greetings of peace[a] to you, ²⁴and so does Mark,[b] Aristarchus,[c] Demas,[d] and Luke, my companions in this ministry.

²⁵May the unconditional love[e] of the Lord Jesus, the Anointed One, be with your spirit![f]

---

a 23 The cultural greeting of that day would be peace or "shalom."

b 24 That is, "John Mark." See Acts 15:36–40. This shows that John Mark was fully restored in his relationship and partnership with the apostle Paul. Since Mark's death was in Alexandria in AD 62, the book of Philemon was obviously written before then. This is the only place in the New Testament that records Mark and Luke being in the same place. Paul had two Gospel writers who traveled with him.

c 24 *Aristarchus* means "best prince" ("ruler"). He was also known as Aristarchus of Thessalonica and is identified in church history as one of the seventy whom Jesus sent out. He was both a ministry companion of Paul and Paul's "fellow prisoner" (Col. 4:10).

d 24 *Demas* means "governor of the people." Demas would later desert Paul and turn back to the world. See 2 Tim. 4:10.

e 25 Or "grace."

f 25 The Aramaic adds a postscript: "End of the letter of Philemon, which was written from Rome and sent by the hands of Onesimus."

YOUR PERSONAL INVITATION

TO FOLLOW JESUS

We can all find ourselves in dark places needing some light—light that brings direction, healing, vision, warmth, and hope. Jesus said, "I am light to the world, and those who embrace me will experience life-giving light, and they will never walk in darkness" (John 8:12). Without the light and love of Jesus, this world is truly a dark place and we are lost forever.

Love unlocks mysteries. As we love Jesus, our hearts are unlocked to see more of his beauty and glory. When we stop defining ourselves by our failures, but rather as the ones whom Jesus loves, our hearts begin to open to the breathtaking discovery of the wonder of Jesus Christ.

All that is recorded in the Scriptures is there so that you will fully believe that Jesus is the Son of God, and that through your faith in him you will experience eternal life by the power of his name (see John 20:31).

If you want this light and love in your life, say a prayer like this—whether for the first time or to express again your passionate desire to follow Jesus:

Jesus, you are the light of the world. I want to follow you, passionately and wholeheartedly. But my sins have separated me from you. Thank you for your love for me. Thank you for paying the price for my sins. I trust your finished work on the cross for my rescue. I turn away from the thoughts and deeds that have separated me from you. Forgive me and

awaken me to love you with all my heart, mind,
soul, and strength. I believe God raised you from the
dead, and I want that new life to flow through me
each day and for eternity. God, I give you my life.
Fill me with your Spirit so that my life will honor you
and I can fulfill your purpose for me. Amen.

You can be assured that what Jesus said about those
who choose to follow him is true: "If you embrace my
message and believe in the One who sent me, you will
never face condemnation, for in me, you have already
passed from the realm of death into the realm of eternal life!" (John 5:24). But there's more! Not only are you
declared "not guilty" by God because of Jesus, you are
also considered his most intimate friend (John 15:15).

As you grow in your relationship with Jesus, continue
to read the Bible, communicate with God through prayer,
spend time with others who follow Jesus, and live out
your faith daily and passionately. God bless you!

ABOUT THE
TRANSLATOR

Brian Simmons is known as a passionate lover of God. After a dramatic conversion to Christ, Brian knew that God was calling him to go to the unreached people of the world and present the gospel of God's grace to all who would listen. With his wife, Candice, and their three children, he spent nearly eight years in the tropical rain forest of the Darien Province of Panama as a church planter, translator, and consultant. Having been trained in linguistics and Bible translation principles, Brian assisted in the Paya-Kuna New Testament translation project, and after their ministry in the jungle, Brian was instrumental in planting a thriving church in New England (U.S.). He is the lead translator for The Passion Translation Project and travels full time as a speaker and Bible teacher. He has been happily married to Candice since 1971 and boasts regularly of his three children and eight grandchildren.

Follow The Passion Translation at:

Facebook.com/passiontranslation
Twitter.com/tPtBible
Instagram.com/passiontranslation

For more information about the translation project please visit:

ThePassionTranslation.com

Encounter the Heart of God

The Passion Translation is a modern, easy-to-read Bible translation that unlocks the passion of God's heart and expresses his fiery love—merging emotion and life-changing truth. This translation will evoke an overwhelming response in every reader, unfolding the deep mysteries of Scripture. If you are hungry for God, The Passion Translation will help you encounter his heart and know him more intimately. Fall in love with God all over again.

The Passion Translation®
The New Testament with Psalms, Proverbs, and Song of Songs
2020 Edition

Available in a variety of styles, including pearlescent hardcover, faux leather, fabric hardcover, standard, compact, and large print.

NEW FEATURES

- Over 1000 new and revised in-depth footnotes with insightful study notes, commentary, word studies, cross references, and alternate translations
- Updated text
- 16 pages of full-color maps

STANDARD FEATURES

- Extensive introductions
- Contemporary font in traditional two-column format
- Premium Bible paper stitched together with layflat Smyth-sewn binding
- Ribbon marker

THE PASSION
TRANSLATION

The Passion Translation®
The New Testament with Psalms, Proverbs, and Song of Songs
2020 Edition

STANDARD HARDCOVER

Ivory

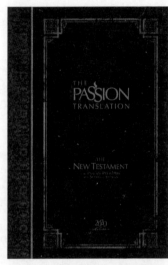

Espresso

Peony

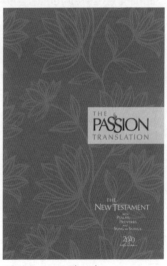

Floral

The Passion Translation®
The New Testament with Psalms, Proverbs, and Song of Songs
2020 Edition

STANDARD FAUX LEATHER

Black

Brown

Gray

Violet

The Passion Translation®
The New Testament with Psalms, Proverbs, and Song of Songs
2020 Edition

STANDARD FABRIC HARDCOVER

Berry Blossom

Passion in Plum

Also available in

LARGE PRINT FAUX LEATHER
Black
Brown
Burgundy
Navy
Violet

COMPACT FAUX LEATHER
Charcoal
Navy
Fuchsia
Violet
Brown
Teal

NOTES

_____

_____

_____

_____

_____

_____

_____

_____

_____

_____

_____

_____

_____

_____

_____

_____

_____

_____

ThePassionTranslation.com